Management for Professionals

For further volumes:
http://www.springer.com/series/10101

Justyna Patalas-Maliszewska

Managing Knowledge Workers

Value Assessment, Methods, and Application Tools

 Springer

Justyna Patalas-Maliszewska
University of Zielona Góra
Zielona Góra
Poland

ISSN 2192-8096   ISSN 2192-810X (electronic)
ISBN 978-3-642-36599-7 ISBN 978-3-642-36600-0 (eBook)
DOI 10.1007/978-3-642-36600-0
Springer Heidelberg New York Dordrecht London

Library of Congress Control Number: 2013935212

Printed on acid-free paper

Springer is part of Springer Science+Business Media (www.springer.com)

Preface

Knowledge management is promoted as an important factor for organizational survival and the maintenance of competitive strength. It has become a necessary condition for enterprises in allowing them to survive in a competitive environment. Enterprises that invest in knowledge, innovation, and systems of work are more likely to achieve a competitive advantage because of the readiness of their workers to learn and achieve and also thanks to effective information and communication transfers.

In intellectual capital management theory and in economic practice, there is a continuous search for methods of measuring intellectual capital (IC). However, there is still no universally accepted method for solving the fundamental problems related to IC value assessment in an enterprise and providing a reliable system for evaluating intangible assets.

Managing knowledge workers is not an easy task. This study focuses on understanding the strategic role of knowledge workers in companies, especially innovative companies. I propose a method and a decision-making model for assessing the value of strategic knowledge resources in companies – the Sknowinnov method.

Decision making is the process of preparing alternative options and selecting one of them for further implementation. The Sknowinnov method provides a feasible solution for new knowledge worker selection because of the way it deals with decision making.

The decision about selecting a new knowledge worker is usually based on forecasts of the potential benefits arising from his or her employment in an enterprise. There is at present a lack of tools for the employee selection process for an innovative company. The primary task is to find knowledge workers that will allow a company to achieve a desired level of innovation.

The problem is therefore clear. A tool that supports the knowledge worker selection process for an innovative company must be found. Building a decision-making model for assessing the value of strategic knowledge resources using the Sknowinnov method allows the right knowledge worker to be found for a company.

The Sknowinnov method introduced in this book offers additional possibilities in the area of knowledge profitability. Apart from calculating investment profitability, this approach appears to be an excellent tool for economic knowledge analysis. The suggested IT tool for supporting decision making at a strategic level with regard to the profitability of any investment in employee qualifications and skills (based on collected data) can identify particular determinants required by an innovative company. It thus allows the rationality and effectiveness of knowledge to be assessed. As a consequence, this method allows knowledge to be evaluated.

I hope that this work will contribute to existing knowledge about the strategic management of intellectual capital in companies and the importance of innovation in gaining a competitive advantage. I trust that this work will prove both practically and theoretically useful with regard to the organization and management of an enterprise.

I wish to thank Prof. Irene Krebs (Brandenburg University of Technology Cottbus) for her dedicated assistance in this study and other aspects of my academic life. I wish to thank Prof. Hannes Werthner (Vienna University of Technology) for making my stay at the Vienna University of Technology stimulating, productive, and enjoyable. I am also grateful to Prof. Tadeusz Krupa and Prof. Kazimierz Perechuda for their insightful and constructive comments on the final draft of the manuscript.

Acknowledgements

Research results included in this work was supported by the Community under a Seventh Framework Programme: People, Marie Curie Intra-European Fellowship for Career Development: "SKnowInnov (Nr: 235585)".

Author:
Dr. Justyna Patalas-Maliszewska
University of Zielona Góra
Institute of Computer Science and Production Management
ul. Licealna 9
65-238 Zielona Góra
e-mail: j.patalas@iizp.uz.zgora.pl

Contents

Introduction

1

1.1 Objectives and Research Problem

The respect and adoption of each employee's intelligence is the key to continuous company management (Davenport and Prusak 1998). Polanyi (1958) divided knowledge into tacit knowledge and explicit knowledge based on the degree of expression. Nonaka and Takeuchi (1995) defined knowledge as a kind of personal characteristic that is too abstract to transfer or even express using words. According to the professional level, Quinn et al. (1996) categorized knowledge into know-what, know-how, know-why, and care-why. In the case of strategic-knowledge management, anticipative capacity building is key to preparing and developing domestic and international cadres of strategic personnel for all sectors—public, nonprofit, and profit (Schein 1995; Argyris and Schon 1996). Howells (1996) thought that knowledge was a kind of expertise that was not editable.

Nowadays, enterprises perceive knowledge as a strategic resource that contributes to their competitive dominance. The term "knowledge worker" seems to have started appearing after 1973 when Peter Drucker (1973) first presented it. However, a clear definition has not yet been established. Thomas H. Davenport (2005) offered this description: "knowledge workers have high degrees of expertise, education, or experience, and the primary purpose of their jobs involves the creation, distribution, or application of knowledge." Thus, describing knowledge workers as strategic-knowledge resources is motivated by the following: the concept of effective management of resources in an organization (Sirmon and Hitt 2003); an enterprise's unique potential in the form of knowledge and experience (Barney 1995); and the concept of competence management (Hamel and Prahalad 1994). A strategic-knowledge resource in a company represents the knowledge, skills, and capabilities of the individuals who constitute the company's workforce. Such resources are usually reflected in a person's education, experience, and specific identifiable skills (Hitt et al. 2001). Yet how can resources be managed to create added value for enterprise?

J. Patalas-Maliszewska, *Managing Knowledge Workers*, Management for Professionals, DOI 10.1007/978-3-642-36600-0_1, © Springer-Verlag Berlin Heidelberg 2013

It is the aim of this monograph to produce a new concept of managing knowledge workers. This research is centered on examining knowledge workers as a group of "specialists in selling" (the model of the so-called knowledge worker-oriented company) and creating a method and decision-making model for assessing the value of strategic-knowledge resources. In particular, empirical research was carried out among innovative companies that conform to the model of such enterprises. A piece of software-"A Consulting IT-system for Knowledge Investment Effects in Companies"—is currently being developed by me based on the designed method for evaluating the effectiveness of investment in knowledge workers in a company and based also on the results gained from questionnaires.

The object of this research was to build a concept of managing knowledge workers. The goals are as follows:

- Defining concepts and models for knowledge-oriented companies.
- Defining the intellectual capital in such companies.
- Defining knowledge workers as a group of specialists in selling.
- Defining employee planning and assessment in knowledge-oriented companies.
- Creating a method for planning and assessing knowledge workers toward increasing innovation within a company.
- Creating a system and decision-making model for assessing knowledge workers for increasing innovation within a company.

The above objectives were conducted by means of an analysis of the following literature:

- Studies dealing with knowledge management and intellectual capital management in companies.
- Studies concerning knowledge workers in company management.
- Studies concerning employee planning and assessment in companies.

I then conducted research into developing methods for planning and assessing knowledge workers with regard to increasing innovation in a company:

- The structure of a knowledge worker-oriented company was defined: knowledge workers form a group of specialists in selling.
- A personnel usefulness function for each m-th knowledge worker in a company was created.
- Empirical studies were conducted among companies.
- An indicator matrix was constructed to assess the effectiveness and efficiency of investment in knowledge workers.
- The group method data handling (GMDH) algorithm was defined, which allows the value of knowledge workers to be determined related to the characteristics of innovation.

My research addressed the following issue. A company has a defined area of operations, and an innovative company has set qualification criteria. There is a set of values related to strategic resources of knowledge (knowledge workers form a group of specialists in selling) in a given company. A method is needed to assess the efficiency in choosing knowledge workers and that will allow the following question to be answered: Is it possible to find an employee who will help a company achieve a desired level of innovation?

This problem can be presented in the form of the following tasks:

1. Available information: the characteristics of a knowledge worker-oriented company with a defined area of operation and a defined value of strategic knowledge resources (knowledge workers). The answer to the following question is sought: How should an algorithm be developed that will allow the qualifying criteria for an innovative company to be connected to the value of strategic knowledge resources?

2. Available information: empirical analyses of the level of innovation in a company (the value of the qualifying criteria for an innovative company). A decision-making model has to be developed to allow the company to make an objective choice of knowledge workers appropriate for the company's innovation needs.

The research problem about finding an algorithm that will enable the qualifying criteria for an innovative company to be connected to strategic knowledge resource is an issue of decision making. The solution may be presented in the form of the following tasks: (1) the possibility of an objective: (a) the model for a knowledge worker-oriented company—the functional areas of the company and the structure of business processes related to those areas; (b) the values of strategic-knowledge resources within a given company; (c) the value of determinants that describe an innovative company; (2) the possibility of assessing the level of innovation in a company according to the value of strategic-knowledge resources.

To solve the research problem, a polynomial decision-making model was designed. It consists of three elements: (1) a base of the values of strategic knowledge resource and the values of criteria that describe an innovative company; (2) a GMDH algorithm; and (3) an analyzer of a logical model and an answer generator.

1.2   Research Hypotheses

Following a study of the literature and observing business practices, the following research hypotheses were adopted. I aim to analyze the effect of knowledge worker selection on the innovation level in a company. In particular, the likely consequences on innovation determinants are studied.

H1: Assessment of a knowledge worker enhances the innovation level of a company.

H2: Selection of a knowledge worker enhances the innovation level of a company.

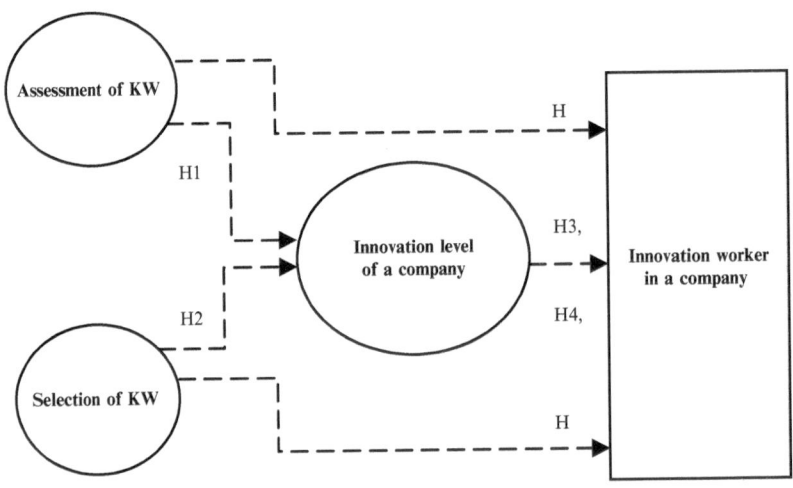

H3. Assessment of a knowledge worker has a direct effect on the innovation level of a company.

H3a. Assessment of a knowledge worker has a direct effect on the quantitative criteria of an innovative company.

H4. Selection of a knowledge worker has a direct effect on the innovation level of a company.

H4a. Selection of a knowledge worker has a direct effect on the quantitative criteria of an innovative company.

H5. Assessment of a knowledge worker has an indirect effect on transforming knowledge workers to innovation workers through an increase in innovation capacity.

H6. Selection of a knowledge worker has an indirect effect on transforming knowledge workers to innovation workers through an increase in innovation capacity.

Knowledge within a company is strongly influenced by the quality and type of formal education possessed by its employees (Janz and Peters 2002; Teixeira and Fortuna 2006; Engelbrecht 1997). Intellectual capital plays a special role in the innovation process. In that sense, it may be appropriate to define innovation workers as a subset of knowledge workers. Innovation workers are defined as those individuals who have better-developed insight than other knowledge workers.

1.3   Scope of Research

In a company, knowledge workers need to acquire a variety of knowledge (information) about their tasks (Drucker 1988). Knowledge management in a company includes the following (Morawski 2006): (1) human resource issues—selection, development, motivation, and evaluation of knowledge workers; (2) structural and organizational issues—selecting appropriate solutions for a flexible structure, the degree of formalization and centralization of effective flow of knowledge and information; (3) organizational culture issues—knowledge-sharing behavior; and (4) strategy issues—locating and acquiring knowledge from the environment.

I believe that it is crucial to develop efficiency in managing knowledge workers and to develop the innovation level of a company. The rationale for undertaking this research is related to the dynamic growth and development of knowledge workers in businesses and the lack of in-depth studies related to this problem.

The research design therefore has a cognitive dimension and application. The first dimension is in terms of contributing to the diagnosis of organizational models based on knowledge and assessing knowledge workers such that a company can raise its level of innovation. The second dimension is in model selection and assessment of knowledge worker; it involves creating a tool for making an objective selection of knowledge workers toward increasing a company's innovation.

The substantive scope of this work includes cross-processing and a subjective approach; it involves creating a holistic view of the methods of managing knowledge workers for innovative companies. The study sought to answer the following questions as specific objectives:

- What are the conventional methods and tools for employee selection and assessment?
- What are the tools for selecting knowledge workers?
- How can the value of knowledge workers be determined?
- What level of innovation in enterprises can result from selecting knowledge workers?
- How can a relationship be formulated between the value of knowledge workers and the level of business innovation?
- How can knowledge workers be transformed into innovation workers?

References

Argyris, C., & Schon, D. (1996). *Organizational learning II*. New York: Addison-Wesley.

Barney, J. B. (1995). Looking inside for competitive advantage. *Academy of Management Perspectives, 9*(4), 49–61.

Davenport, T. H. (2005). *Thinking for a living, how to get better performance and results from knowledge workers*. Boston: Harvard Business School Press.

Davenport, T. H., & Prusak, L. (1998). *Working knowledge: How organizations manage what they know*. Bostan: Harvard Business School Press.

Drucker, P. F. (1973). *Management: Tasks, responsibilities, practices*. New York: Harper Row.

Drucker, P. F. (1988). The coming of the new organization. *Harvard Business Review, 88105*, 01–02.

Engelbrecht, H. J. (1997). International R&D spillovers, human capital and productivity in OECD economies: An empirical investigation. *European Economic Review, 41*, 1479–1488.

Hamel, G., & Prahalad, C. (1994). *Competing for the future*. Boston: Harvard Business School Press.

Hitt, M. A., Bierman, L., Shimizu, K., & Kochhar, R. (2001). Direct and moderating effects of human capital on strategy and performance in professional service firms: A resource-based perspective. *Academy of Management Journal, 44*, 13–28.

Howells, J. (1996). Tacit knowledge, innovation and technology transfer. *Technology Analysis and Strategic Management, 8*(2), 91–106.

Janz, N., & Peters, B. (2002). *Innovation and innovation success in the German manufacturing sector, econometric evidence at firm level*. Mannheim: Centre for European Economic Research (ZEW), Department of Industrial Economics and International Management.

Morawski, M. (2006). *Zarządzanie Wiedzą. Organizacja-System-Pracownik (Knowledge management. Organisation-System-Employee)*. Wroclaw: Economical University.

Nonaka, L., & Takeuchi, H. (1995). *The knowledge-creating company*. New York: Oxford University Press.

Polanyi, M. (1958). *The tacit dimension*. New York: ME Sharp.

Quinn, J. B., Anderson, P., & Finkelstein, S. (1996). Managing professional intellect: Making the most of the best. *Harvard Business Review*, Mar–Apr, pp. 71–80.

Schein, E. (1995). *Organizational culture and leadership*. San Francisco: Jossey-Bass.

Sirmon, D., & Hitt, M. A. (2003). Managing resources: Linking unique resources, management and wealth creation in family firms. *Entrepreneurship Theory and Practice, 27*, 339–358.

Teixeira, A. A. C., & Fortuna, N. (2006). Human capital, trade and long-run productivity. Testing the technological absorption hypothesis for the Portuguese economy, 1960–2001. FEP Working Papers: 226

Enterprises functioning in a market economy have to implement changes in their systems of organization and the management they use. In economic practice, making a decision in an enterprise is conditioned by competitors' actions and changing environmental factors, e.g., technical progress and the results of research efforts. Added value for a company can be determined as knowledge, employees' skills and abilities, social relations, know-how, and, particularly, effective investment in intellectual capital. Enterprises that invest in human capital and systems of work achieve a competitive advantage because of their workers' readiness to learn and achieve and also thanks to effective information and communication transfers (Edvinsson and Malone 1997).

Knowledge management is promoted as an important and necessary factor for organizational survival and maintenance of competitive strength. To remain at the forefront, organizations need a good capacity to retain, develop, organize, and utilize their employees' capabilities.

It has long been recognized that "the increase in the stock of useful knowledge and the extension of its application are the essence of modern economic growth" (Kuznets 1966; Ackoff 1974). Poland is an example of a country that is transforming itself into a knowledge-based economy. This process of change comes as a response to the country's developmental progress on the basis of export-led growth and the input of multinational companies.

At present, the advantage of any company is determined by the effectiveness and extent of the knowledge that its workers possess combined with their level of involvement within the company. The role of intellectual-capital management mainly consists of striving to increase the share of non-material resources (at the cost of material ones) in the generated products, services, and the total market value of an organization (Król and Ludwiczyński 2007). Knowledge, based on information and supported by cultural values, has become an independent force and the single most decisive factor in social, economic, technological, and cultural transformation. Enterprises that invest in knowledge, innovation, and systems of work often achieve a competitive advantage as a result of their workers' readiness to

J. Patalas-Maliszewska, *Managing Knowledge Workers*, Management for Professionals,
DOI 10.1007/978-3-642-36600-0_2, © Springer-Verlag Berlin Heidelberg 2013

learn and achieve. Additionally, such competitive advantages are often formed as a consequence of effective information and communication transfers.

A number of potential benefits and challenges with implementing knowledge management in companies are outlined in this part of the monograph. The key research questions include the following:

- What is a knowledge-based economy and why has this topic become an issue?
- What are the known models of organizational structures in knowledge-oriented companies?
- What are the development trends of knowledge-oriented companies?
- Why should companies adopt models of organizational structures of knowledge-oriented companies?

2.1   Essence of Knowledge Management

2.1.1   Defining the Knowledge-Based Economy

According to the Organisation for Economic Co-operation and Development (OECD), a knowledge-based economy signifies one directly based on the production, distribution, and use of knowledge and information (OECD 1996). At the OECD conference on employment and growth in the knowledge-based economy, Foray and Lundvall joined forces, arguing that the "economy is more strongly and more directly rooted in the production, distribution and use of knowledge than ever before" (Foray and Lundvall 1996). According to other authors, however, the concept of a knowledge-based economy is rather a rhetorical term, a metaphor "often used in a superficial and uncritical way" (Smith and Barfield 1996; Smith 2002).

The knowledge-based economy has allowed a rapid integration of enormous intellectual resources of economies in transition into the European intellectual pool, stimulating the development of those countries. All countries can benefit from developing a knowledge-based economy toward becoming a more equal participant in the global development process. The four pillars of the knowledge-based economy are defined as:

- An economic and industrial regime
- An educated and skilled population
- A dynamic information infrastructure
- An effective innovation system

Concepts for a knowledge-based economy do not fall into a single, universally accepted definition. What follows is a brief review of selected approaches that may be used toward forming a definition.

Drucker stated that a knowledge-based economy is "an economic order in which knowledge, not labor, raw materials or capital, is a key resource, a social order, for which inequality based on knowledge is a major challenge and the system in which the government cannot solve social and economic problems" (Drucker 1994).

According to a report prepared jointly by the OECD and the World Bank in 2000, a knowledge-based economy is one in which "knowledge is created, absorbed and utilized more effectively by enterprises, organizations, individuals and communities, promoting rapid economic development" (Dahlman and Andersson 2000).

Koźmiński defines a knowledge-based economy as one in which there are many businesses based on knowledge and an understanding of their respective competitive advantages (Koźmiński 2002).

In the government document entitled "e-Poland—An Agenda for the Information Society in Poland in 2001–2006," a knowledge-based economy is defined as "an economy in which knowledge is a major factor in productivity and economic growth (before labor and capital, raw materials and energy), a key role in knowledge-based economy is played by information, education and technology, especially information and communication technologies" (The Ministry of Economy 2001).

To illustrate the Polish position as compared with that of other countries in creating conditions for the development of a knowledge-based economy, it is appropriate to present the index value of the knowledge economy in the European Union (EU) and the United States (Fig. 2.1). This is done in accordance with the Knowledge Assessment Methodology (KAM)—an interactive method of diagnosing the state of a knowledge-based economy developed by the World Bank.

The relatively low value of the index for Poland compelled me to undertake research in the field of managing company knowledge.

2.1.2 Companies in a Knowledge-Based Economy

The aforementioned organizational structures provide a forum for representatives of science, modern industry, and all aspects of entrepreneurship. The main purpose of these structures is to bring research results (and research scientists) and innovative solutions closer to the social and economic practices of enterprises. The activities of such organizations are aimed at developing new technologies and upgrading existing ones and finding solutions to synthetic, technological, and analytical problems encountered by various active companies.

Nevertheless, the range and speed of innovation enterprises is restricted compared with that of large enterprises, which typically have their own research and development infrastructure and the financial means to allow extensive research (Amit and Zott 2001). "Innovation is not a guarantee of success, it is a chance … leading companies develop the wallet of innovation, which others can take from in order to sustain their own growth" (Davila et al. 2006).

For knowledge and expertise to be useful to an organization, they must be applicable to those organizational strategic objectives that add the most value, such as customer service, market leadership, and operational effectiveness (Zack 1999). In this context, the term "intellectual capital" (or intellectual resources) is often used to represent knowledge that can be converted into profit and other forms of value (Stewart 1998).

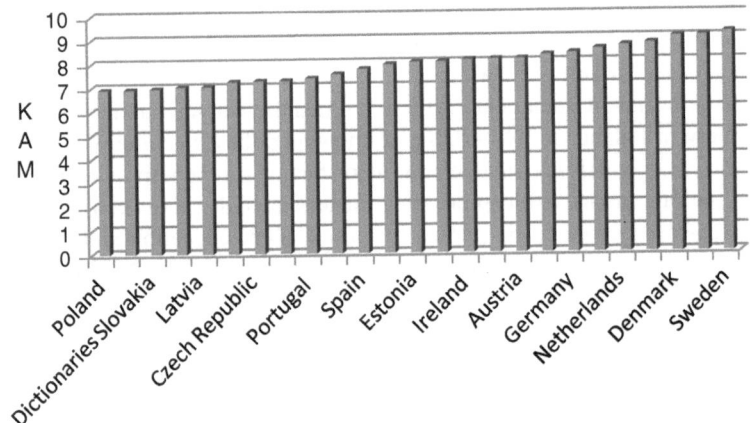

Fig. 2.1 Index level of the knowledge economy in the EU and the United States in 2006 (Source: Żelazny 2006)

In the knowledge economy, it is necessary to take into account innovation, education, information, communication, and knowledge management at a level that are appropriate for the organization. Such knowledge management should also take into account aspects of the institutional and business environment and any regional policy features that may have an effect on the enterprise (Grudzewski and Hejduk 2004). In this light, I define the determinants of the company in the knowledge economy as indicated in Fig. 2.2.

Based on previous these findings, it can be determined that the task of policy innovation is to use any appropriate innovative methods of analysis, innovation, and decision making and then become the main force of the creative organization. As such, these methods should be regarded as assets under its management system and company culture. In the literature (Drucker 1994; Pisano and Wheelwright 1995), an innovative enterprise is characteristically defined as one that has high competence, an ability to generalize and innovate, apply policies, is customer-oriented, possesses all appropriate information, and is flexible in a changing market environment.

Action in terms of an enterprise's development and the integration of knowledge and innovation are important factors in developing a competitive advantage (Pisano and Wheelwright 1995). The literature is distinguished by a number of definitions of the concept of innovation, such as the following. "Innovation refers to goods, services or ideas that are perceived as new. The idea may have long been, but it represents an innovation for the person who sees it as the new" (Kotler 1994). "Innovation is all that is perceived by humans as new, independent of objective news" (Rogers 1995). According to the theories of Drucker, "A source of

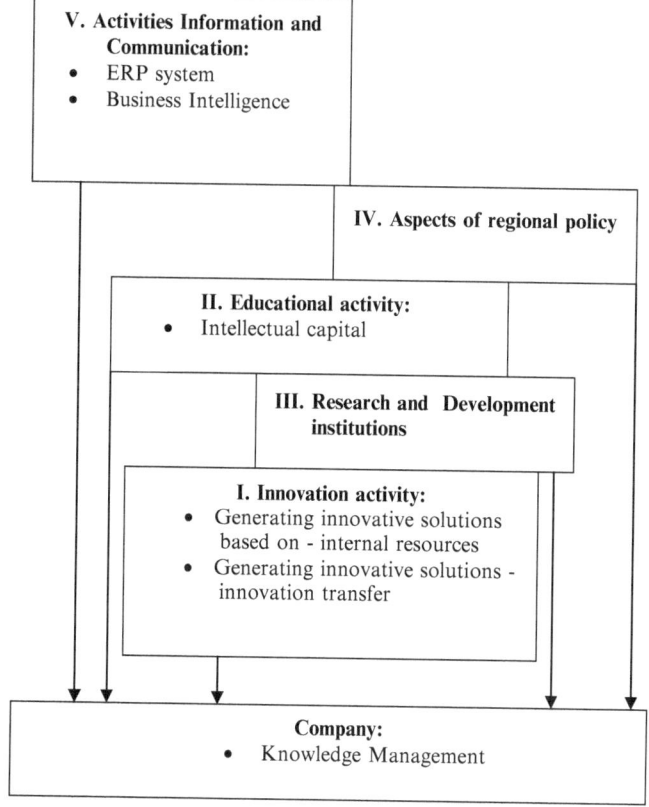

Fig. 2.2 Determinants of the company in the knowledge economy

innovation is the observation of market processes and the implementation of innovation which allows the company to gain a competitive advantage in the market" (Drucker 1994).

For a company to achieve sustainable competitiveness, it should seek to obtain support from research institutions with the aim of acquiring knowledge and innovation as "drivers of growth" (according to the document "Working together for growth and jobs-A new start for the Lisbon Strategy"). Companies should develop themselves as attractive business partners through the thoughtful use of patents, technology, location, quality products, and low-cost purchases. A competitive advantage can determine the competitiveness of a company. Competitiveness is a concept that has a high degree of theoretical abstraction.

Thus, there is a clear set of dominant competitive strategies:
- Cost leadership
- Creation of uniqueness for the client
- Being competitive with regard to deadlines
- Developing key competences

- Gaining an advantage through collaboration
- Competing for the future
  There are also sub-competitive strategies:
- Potential competitiveness-the full range of the organization's resources
- Competitive advantage-understood to be the corollary result of the appropriate use of corporate resources
- Competitive instruments-measures aimed at achieving the organization's competitive position
- The competitive position—a leading position of the organization in its field of industry

In the literature, innovation is commonly defined as the ability and incentive to explore and commercially exploit any scientific research, new concepts, or ideas that could improve the competitive position of a company (Prahalad and Hamel 1990). It is clearly noted, however, that most companies do not have the power and resources necessary to build a truly innovative company owing to their limited structure and size. Hence it seems logical that companies should collaborate with R&D institutions to become innovative. This cooperation will allow the creation of joint projects and new technical knowledge in the companies' area of expertise. Innovative companies should lead to a system of general creation that diffuses into the economy (OECD 1996).

Highly innovative companies, however, are not necessarily guaranteed continued economic growth. There remains a constant risk of failure as a result of putting resources into activities that may lead to innovation. Among other factors, financial resources-or a lack thereof-usually represent the main obstacle to growth. Today, however, in Europe at least, financial barriers are no longer such a key factor inhibiting the growth of a company because there are possibilities of obtaining funding from the EU.

2.1.3   Competitive Advantage in the Knowledge Economy

Building competitive advantage through dynamic capability requires constant knowledge flow within and outside the organization and a continuously updated knowledge repository. To be competitive in the knowledge-based economy, companies need to base their activities on cooperation with R&D centers, universities, and networks of firms. By highlighting the trends in the organizational structures of enterprises and using a defined network economy as a base, the following organizational solutions can be identified (Teece 2002; Stabryła 2009):

- A local, international, and global network
- A virtual organization
- Teleworking
- The individual inventor and stand-alone laboratory
- Highly flexible Silicon Valley-type firms
- Conglomerates
- Alliances

2.1.3.1 Local, International, and Global Networks

This organizational structure is based on the mutual relations of the unrelated business capital of a cooperative. These entities are related to IT technologies. Such networks may be characterized as follows (Butra et al. 1999):

- Combination potential-the ability to achieve various objectives in different conditions of business
- Activation of a network-the distribution of powers to induce new forms of cooperation. The composition of the network can be modified in line with a particular strategy. In this regard, we can distinguish the following types of network activation-controlled, monitored, and distributed
- A consistency network-determining the density of ties among network members
There are four basic types of networks:
- Stars-consisting of leading companies
- Connection hubs-where all parties are equal
- Temporary networks-weak and formal
- Regional-usually an expression of territorial cooperation
Furthermore, it is even possible to categorize the scope of the networks:
- Local-between a home country and its adjoining neighbors
- International-among several countries
- Global-operators in almost all countries of the world
Local networks are formed between companies or between companies and the business environment.

2.1.3.2 Virtual Organization

Virtual organizations have the capacity to be very creative and to excel at early-stage innovation activities. If they do indeed establish a strong alliance with a competent manufacturer, they may also have the capacity to be the first to market, despite their lack of the requisite internal capabilities.

In the literature, there are many definitions of virtual organizations. Such definitions include a temporary network of independent companies-suppliers, customers, competitors, and the combined IT skills to share costs and gain access to new possibilities (Byrne et al. 1993). Virtual organizations are also defined as an artificial creation that, through the maximum usefulness to the customer, is based on an individual competence base and focuses on pursuing the integration of independent enterprises in chain-making processes (Schulz 1996). Virtual organizations are described by Mowshowitz (1997) as having the following characteristics:

- Analyzing abstract needs or requirements
- Needing an analysis and determination of methods for their implementation
- Adopting the dynamic adaptation of methods to deal with their needs
- Researching and analyzing the methods adopted for implementation in conjunction with the needs of participants and customers in their network of operations

For enterprises to gain a competitive advantage through a virtual organizational structure, they must meet the following conditions (Zimniewicz 2000):

- Be competent

- Be able to cooperate with other actors
- Have modern communications and IT

In designing a modern innovative network, the following questions need to be answered:

- What will be the added value for users?
- What form of network should be adopted?
- What communication technologies does the network offer?
- What entities should be co-regulated under contracts?
- Should cooperation be based on mutual trust rather than formal cooperation?
- What organizational structures will the network management unit possess?
- What role should R&D institutes have?
- What will be the financial arrangements in cooperating through a network?
- What will be the form, structure, and content of the datasets in the network?
- What will be the form, structure, and content of the database results from the participation?

Enterprises have limited access to collaboration with R&D that aims at identifying, implementing, and disseminating innovation. Virtual enterprises, however, may provide opportunities for innovation. Via network connections, virtual enterprises have access to other companies and can base their production capacity on the knowledge that different firms possess and the innovations they want to share. This provides a powerful combination of the effects of several cooperating companies and is related to the breaking down of barriers to a lack of resources: capital, technical and technological bases; human resources, knowledge, and experience.

2.1.3.3 Teleworking

Teleworking is a form of providing work outside company offices where the worker maintains contact with supervisors and colleagues via telecommunications (Nilles 1998). It constitutes a form of employment by the employer, and its main goal is to create opportunities for reducing costs associated with the work of both the employer and employee. The advantages of teleworking from the standpoint of the employer are:

- Reduced expenses associated with the work
- Increased group employee productivity
- No need for constant upgrading of skills
- No need for strict planning and analysis of the use of working time
- Optimization of staffing
- Reductions in organizational conflict
  The advantages of teleworking from the perspective of the employee are:
- Reduced expenditure in commuting
- Independence and flexibility with working hours
- The possibility for the individual to determine their own scope plus the type and pace of work
- Fewer conflicts with colleagues

Thus, teleworking may provide a convenient form of employment for firms. However, it is not without its obvious drawbacks, including:

- No direct supervisory manager
- The need for continuous upgrading of skills
- Irregular working rhythms
- Limited career advancement opportunities
- The difficulty in separating time off from work time
- A sense of alienation
- A potential lack of loyalty

2.1.3.4 Individual Inventor and the Stand-Alone Laboratory

When property rights are weak (the normal case), the inventor's ability to capture value is dramatically circumscribed (Teece 2002). In a case where the individual inventor has a patent but little else, the patent owner's options include the following: licensing the technology to incumbent firms who already have the necessary complementary assets in place; using intellectual property as collateral to raise funds to establish an organization to exploit the technology; or exchanging the intellectual property for cash or equity in an established firm.

The stand-alone research laboratory faces many of the same challenges as the individual inventor. The main difference is that the laboratory can bring multiple organizational skills to bear on the R&D process. Furthermore, the probability of fusing multiple technologies is enhanced by the bringing together of multiple research disciplines.

2.1.3.5 Highly Flexible Silicon Valley–Type Firms

These companies typically have shallow hierarchies and significant local autonomy. Such firms tend to resist the hierarchical accoutrements of seniority and rank found in the above categories, and they resist the functional specialization that restricts following up on ideas and may destroy the sense of commonality of purpose.

2.1.3.6 Conglomerates

In terms of access to capital and diversity of activities, one would not expect a conglomerate to look very different from a stand-alone firm with respect to innovative capacity (Williamson 1975).

2.1.3.7 Alliances

An alliance is a union of several companies that are competitors and operate in the same market; it usually has a long-term nature and the aim is to implement a joint venture. The integral component of an alliance is the sharing of the partners' knowledge and funds for the mutual benefit of all parties involved. This association must have a clearly defined goal, and its chances for survival depend on the balance between the partners. Strategic alliances are typically characterized by three basic features:

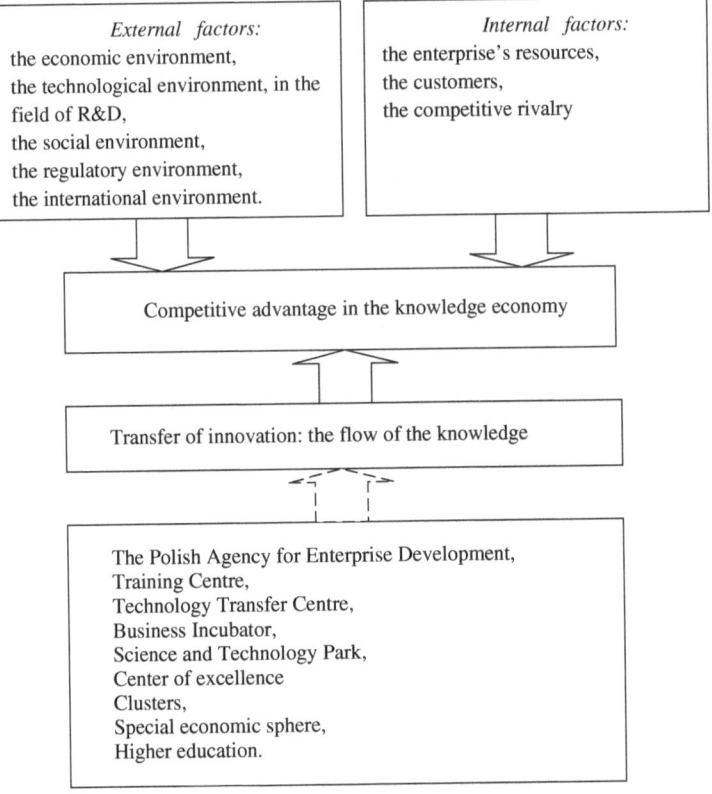

Fig. 2.3 Determinants of competitive advantage in the knowledge economy

- Fragmentation-alliances relate to only a fraction of the participants' contractual duties. Enterprises entering into an alliance may operate individually and outside the bounds of the agreement
- Transfer of assets within the coalition-the partners are committed to providing both material input (including capital and infrastructure) and intangible assets (including knowledge, skills, and abilities) to achieve joint projects
- Integrity-the revision of certain elements of a cooperation agreement cause the amendment of behavior patterns (Kraciuk 2005)

Therefore, on the basis of such descriptions, the following external factors shape the competitive advantage for a company in the knowledge economy (Fig. 2.3):

- Technological development on a global scale
- The possibility of adopting new technologies in the home country
- The overall level of economic development
- Innovation policy in the home country

And there are internal factors (Fig. 2.3):

- Personality factors arising from the business (organizational skills, creativity, desire to stand out, openness to innovation)

- Factors associated with the experience of the entrepreneur
- Factors relating to company personnel
- Factors relating to the close environment
- Factors arising from the company's location (e.g., the possibility of contact with R&D)
- The company's results (sales growth, earnings, liquidity) and any legal considerations relating to the company

A company's functioning in the knowledge economy involves rethinking how the organization creates value from a knowledge-centric perspective and redesigning and orchestrating the role of intellectual assets in the firm's strategy. To manage its knowledge more systematically, the enterprise must devise an agenda for transforming itself from an organization that simply comprises knowledgeable individuals to a knowledge-focused organization. Such an organization stewards the creation and sharing of knowledge within and across internal business functions and orchestrates the flow of know-how to and from external firms.

2.2 Knowledge Management and Managing Intellectual Capital

2.2.1 Essence of Knowledge Management in Organizations

Knowledge can be understood in many ways. The following taxonomy may be useful (Teece 2002):

- Codified/tacit
  Tacit knowledge is that which is difficult to transfer in a meaningful and complete manner. It is slow and costly to transmit.
- Positive/negative knowledge
  A discovery (positive knowledge) can focus research on promising areas of inquiry, thereby avoiding blind alleys.
- Autonomous/systemic knowledge
  Autonomous knowledge is that which yields value without major modifications of the system into which it is adopted.
- Intangible assets, tangible assets, and intellectual property
  Knowledge assets are simply one class of intangible assets; they differ from tangible assets in several important respects (Table 2.1).

Knowledge can be regarded as a resource for the company owing to its characteristics (Jarugowa and Fijałkowska 2002): continuity, simultaneity, nonlinearity, dominant character, and immateriality.

Knowledge is a broad concept, embracing both formalized knowledge (explicit) and non-formal knowledge (hidden). From the relationship among data, information, information management, and knowledge, the latter should be regarded as a strategic resource for a company (Fig. 2.4) (Senn 1990). The application of information systems that support knowledge management in a company may offer guarantees of a constant competitive advantage in the market.

Table 2.1 Differences between intangible and tangible assets

	Knowledge (intangible) assets	Physical (tangible) assets
Publicness	Use by one party need not prevent use by another	Use by one party prevents simultaneous use by another
Depreciation	Does not "wear out", but usually depreciates rapidly	Wear out, may depreciate quickly or slowly
Transfer cost	Hard to calibrate	Easier to calibrate
Property rights	Limited	Generally comprehensive and clearer, at least
Enforcement of property rights	Relatively difficult	Relatively easy

Source: (Teece 2002)

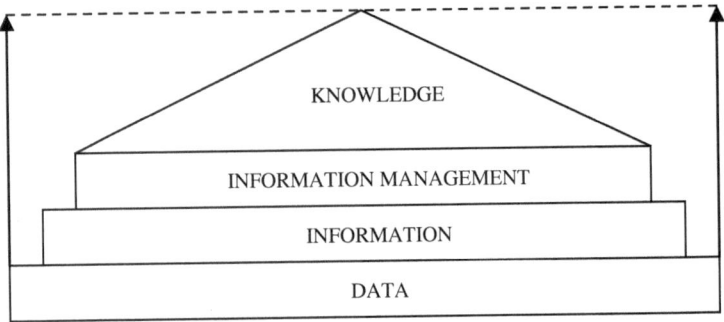

Fig. 2.4 Relationship among data, information, information management, and knowledge (Source: Senn 1990)

The process of knowledge management is defined as follows:

- Building a dynamic work environment and learning to foster the continuous generation, collection, and use of individual and collective knowledge to discover new values for the company (Evans 2005)
- A strictly defined system for identifying, generating, analyzing, addressing, processing, and using information (Kotarba and Kotarba 2003)

Managing knowledge is the emerging model of business with all aspects of knowledge, including knowledge creation, codification, knowledge sharing and using these activities to promote learning and innovation. (Gupta et al. 2004)

Knowledge management is a specially designed process system, and even the art of identifying, generating, analyzing, addressing, processing and the use of information and knowledge in order to make faster, smarter and better decisions in turning knowledge into value for customers. (Ives et al. 1998)

Knowledge management is a logical continuation of the trend in the development of science in organization and management. (Kisielnicki 2004)

Knowledge management is ensuring that knowledge is available to those who need it, in the place, at the time and the form they wish, so that the organization can function effectively in not only in economic terms, but also socially. (Ives et al. 1998)

Knowledge management is the use of resources that the organization probably already has-well-functioning solutions for its information systems management, organizational change and human resources. (Davenport and Prusak 1998)

All of the processes and operations associated with creating, acquiring, extracting, sharing and using knowledge, wherever they would be, in order to increase the efficiency, effectiveness and learning organization. (Swan et al. 1999)

The deliberate and systematic management of knowledge and fundamental processes of its creation, accumulation, arrangement, dissemination and use in achieving the objectives of the organization. (Davenport and Prusak 1998)

All the methods, instruments and tools that assist in the comprehensive terms of the key processes in the sphere of knowledge. (Mertins et al. 2000)

Ways of improving the knowledge mobilization of resources by organizations operating in a turbulent environment in order to continuously follow-on innovation. (Nowell et al. 1996)

Knowledge management is primarily concerned with people and its aim is to achieve such a level of interaction of people that will neutralize the weaknesses and maximize the talents and strengths of the participants in the organization. (Drucker 1994)

Based on the chosen definition of knowledge management, I assume that the process of knowledge management is essentially the process of supporting decision making in an enterprise based on collected data, information, and transferred knowledge.

In the literature there are three approaches in knowledge management: the Japanese approach, the process-based approach, and the resource-based approach.

The Japanese approach (Nonaka and Takeuchi 1995); (Table 2.2): The creation and expansion of knowledge takes place through social interaction between explicit knowledge (knowledge that can be passed on in the form of words, formulas, rules, and symbols) and tacit knowledge (knowledge that is difficult to provide in the form of words, formulas, rules, and symbols).

The Japanese approach assumes that knowledge is acquired by all employees in an organization and that the interactions between employees and the culture of the organization are of particular importance.

The process-based approach: The concept was developed by Davenport and Prusak (Davenport and Prusak 2000). The knowledge-management model is based on three pillars: knowledge expansion, knowledge codification, and transfer of knowledge. According to the model of Davenport and Prusak, knowledge expansion includes four basic steps (Davenport and Prusak 2000):

- Release of resources (consisting of creating R&D centers, whose task is to manage knowledge and acquire new knowledge)
- Acquisition of knowledge (involving the hiring of new employees)
- Internal mergers (involving the linking of individual people or departments, leading to creative solutions)
- Networking (involving the creation of communities and professional networks linking experts from different organizations)

Davenport and Prusak also distinguished two knowledge-management planes: (1) operational, which involves the practical aspects of using knowledge to implement the goals of the business and its operations; (2) strategic, whose mission is to

Table 2.2 The creation and expansion of knowledge

	Tacit knowledge	Explicit knowledge
Tacit knowledge	Socialisation	Externalisation
Explicit knowledge	Internalisation	Combination

Source: (Nonaka and Takeuchi 1995)

build the company as a knowledge-based organization, supporting both obtaining and motivating employees to share and develop knowledge.

The resource-based approach (Leonard-Barton 1995): This approach to knowledge management is based on a model of effective knowledge management known as "sources of knowledge." These elements are as follows: (1) the core competences, consisting of skills and knowledge workers, organizational norms and values, system solutions management and labor, collective problem solving, implementation and integration of new tools and technologies; and (2) experimentation and development to deal with future problems, which involves looking for areas of possible improvement, and importing knowledge from the environment and other organizations. This approach will be examined in greater detail in Sect. 4.1.1.

Knowledge management covers any intentional, systematic process or practice of creating, acquiring, capturing, sharing, and using productive knowledge, wherever it resides, to enhance learning and performance in organizations (Foray 2002). Knowledge management is promoted as being necessary for organizational survival and maintaining competitive strength. To remain at the forefront, organizations need a good capacity to retain, develop, organize, and utilize their employees' capabilities. In an organization, knowledge management relates to the formulation of a strategy in the following sense: deepening knowledge of the organization's mission, developing a power-oriented organizational culture of knowledge, selecting the objectives of knowledge and knowledge strategies to achieve those goals, identifying knowledge gaps and barriers, assessing the knowledge created in the enterprise, implementing knowledge strategies-design tasks, roles, processes, information infrastructure, and computer technology.

With regard to a defined set of knowledge-management elements, the following combination allows a knowledge-management process to be built and implemented in a company:

- Collection of knowledge
- Networks of relationships
- Methods of knowledge transfer
- Information systems
- Information networks
- Semantic systems
- Culture of the organization

The following instruments have been identified as ones that distinguish enterprise knowledge management (Maier et al. 2005; Gimeno 2004; Hambrick and Cannella 2004; Lee and Yang 2000; Lindgren et al. 2004; Lu and Beamish 2004; Picot et al. 1996):

- Maps of knowledge sources
- Competency management
- Individual experience
- Achieved experience
- Good practice
- Managing semantic content

An important part of the methodical knowledge of an organization involves providing a model that integrates knowledge management to ensure the quality of management and the expansion of intellectual capital in that organization. Based on Kotarba and Kotarba (2003), an original model formulated in terms of knowledge-management strategy formulation and implementation in the enterprise appears in Fig. 2.5.

The implementation of this model of knowledge management (Fig. 2.5) in a company requires consistency and understanding the use of two management areas-strategy and knowledge. Knowledge management should be considered another approach to management. Its role is to support strategic management and also to innovate management. Knowledge management in a company always refers to a specific category of management: management functions, level of management, stage of management, and area of management.

2.2.2 Essence of Intellectual Capital Management

With regard to research, the status of knowledge includes methods of intellectual capital assessment based on investment in the staff's knowledge development. Human resource capacity building within a company includes the development of employees with desired characteristics and skills. Such employees can lead to creating increased business performance (value added) and establishing a competitive advantage. Investing in intellectual capital can be more clearly understood in the context of the impact of the educational system on employees (gaining the desired qualifications). The staff resources of enterprises are still seen in terms of costs, rather than as capital.

The value of companies has traditionally been judged on the basis of their financial assets, property, or other tangible assets. Today, competitive advantage is viewed as being based on the knowledge of workers. Such intangibles as brand names, patents, copyrights, and spending on R&D are now a significant part of the assets of many companies.

According to the laws of accounting, intangible assets should include the "rights of property suitable for commercial use, any expected economic life that exceeds one year and the intention of use by the company", in particular:

- Copyrights, related rights, licenses, concessions, rights to inventions, patents
- Trademarks in terms of utility and ornamental appearance
- "Know-how" (Accounting Act)

Intangible assets should also include goodwill and any acquired R&D costs.

In the literature, there are various definitions of intellectual capital (IC).

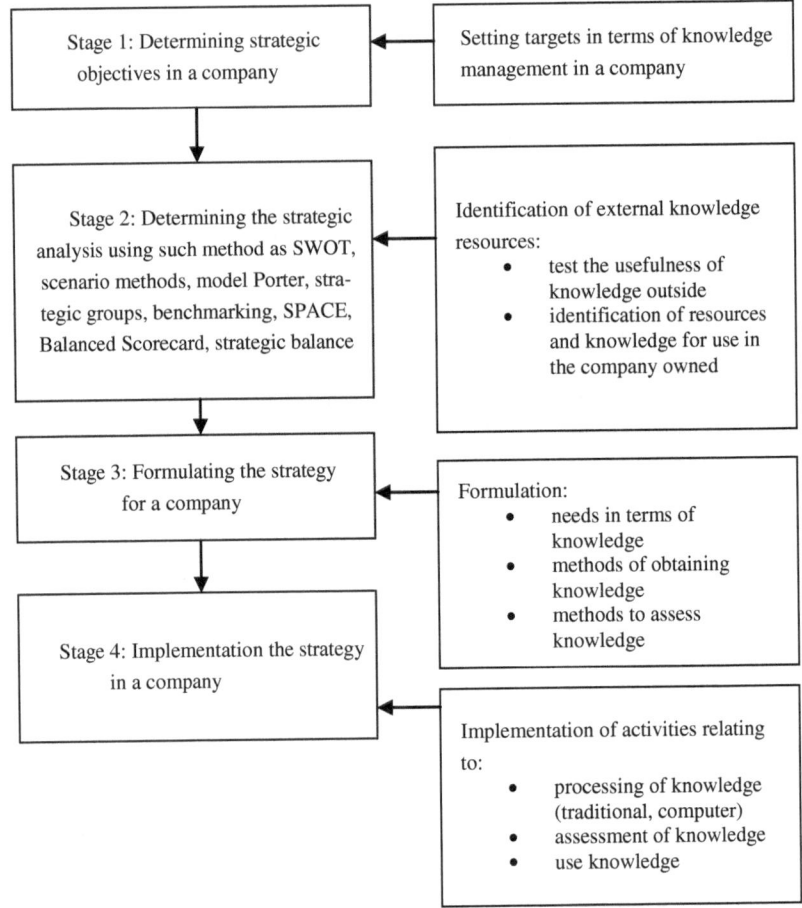

Fig. 2.5 Model of knowledge management in a company related to strategy

> Intellectual capital is knowledge, experience, organizational technology, customer relations and professional skills, which give … a competitive advantage in the market. (Edvinsson and Malone 1997)

> It is knowledge that can be converted. (Jarugowa and Fijałkowska 2002)

Human capital can be said to consist of a collection of the following factors:
- Employee characteristics: intelligence, commitment, energy, positive attitude, integrity, honesty
- The ability of the staff to learn: receptivity, imagination, the ability for analytical thinking, creativity
- Employee motivation in sharing information and knowledge: a team spirit and striving to achieve objectives (Sokołowska 2005)
  Structural capital (also known as organizational capital) consists of intellectual property rights, including patents, licenses, trademarks, and copyrights. It is also the

organizational capacity of a company and includes any physical systems used to transmit and store intellectual material. This involves such factors as the quality and range of information systems, the reputation of the company, the concept of the organization, and its related documentation.

According to Edvinsson and Malone, "Intellectual capital takes three basic forms: human capital, structural capital, and customer capital. Human capital includes knowledge, skills, and abilities of employees. Structural capital is everything in an organization that supports employees (human capital) in their work. Customer capital is the strength and loyalty of customer relations" (Edvinsson and Malone 1997).

According to the Skandia Navigator, the IC of an enterprise may be regarded in terms of at least one of three aspects: its employees, its structure, and its customers. Thus, IC includes human capital, structural capital, and customer capital. And although each of these three types of capital is intangible and reflects the assets belonging to the knowledge of the enterprise, each of them can be assessed and evaluated in terms of investment opportunities (Cascio 2010).

According to Kurowski and Fazlagić, IC consists of:

- Human resources-the overall ability of company employees who provide know-how, a resource that takes into account the collective experience, specialist skills, general skills, and knowledge of employees
- Intellectual assets-descriptions of specific knowledge that the company possesses (the property is not guaranteed or guaranteed by law) and thus can be traded in the form of intangible assets
- Intellectual property-intellectual assets that can be protected (licenses, patents, copyrights, brands, and trade secrets) (Fazlagic and Kurowski 1999)

It is also acknowledged that intellectual assets are a component of IC. Brooking (1996) distinguishes four aspects of IC: market resources (such as brands, customers, distribution channels, customer orders); competence (the ability to solve problems); intellectual property (such as patents, trademarks, copyrights), and infrastructure (such as culture, processes, databases, communication systems). Bonits believes that IC should not include intellectual property (such as patents or copyrights) since it is a component of ordinary assets (Bonits 1998).

Concepts of IC based on an analysis of the literature are presented in Table 2.3.

With regard to common trends among the definitions, it is evident that most of them are divided into the following components of IC:

- Human capital
- Structural capital (organizational)
- Customer capital

An analysis of the definition allows the identification of several common points for describing IC and related concepts:

- IC is based on knowledge
- IC consists of a combination of intangible assets
- IC fills the gap between market value and accounting

I cannot accurately determine the value of IC using the traditional accounting model owing to the nature of IC. The appropriate use of IC can create a solid basis

Table 2.3 Concepts of intellectual capital

Concept of intellectual capital	Source
Monitor intangible assets Intellectual capital: *internal structure + external structure + personal competencies*	Sveiby
Balanced scorecard Intellectual capital: *learning and development perspectives + customers perspectives + financial perspectives*	Kaplan, Norton
Schematic of "Skandia" Intellectual capital: *human capital + structural capital (organizational)*	Edvinsson
Platform values Intellectual capital: *human capital + structural capital (organizational) + customer capital*	Petrash, Edvinsson, Onge, Armstrong, Bukowitz, Williams
Identification of the components of intellectual capital: Intellectual capital: *marketable assets + assets related to the human factor + infrastructure assets + market value*	Brooking
Identification of the components of intellectual capital Intellectual capital: *human capital + structural capital (organizational) + customer capital*	Stewart
Measurements of a company's intellectual capital Intellectual capital: *human capital + structural capital (organizational)*	Ross
Elements of intellectual capital Intellectual capital: *human capital + intellectual assets + intellectual property*	Sullivan

for competitive advantage in the market, but management of IC generally depends on the specific activities of the company and the size of the industry in which it operates.

The relationship between the types of IC is a strategic reflection of the current value of the company. Understanding the nature of intangible assets changes the way business is conducted. Based on reviewed opinions—Table 2.3 concerning the definition of IC, its components can be defined as follows:

1. Human capital:
   - Traits added by an employee-intelligence, involvement, energy, positive attitude, reliability, honesty.
   - The employee's ability to learn-the power to absorb information, imagination, analytical thinking, creativity, employee's motivation in sharing information and knowledge, the ability to work in a team and engage in self-motivation to pursue and achieve goals
2. Structural (organizational) capital-intellectual copyrights, including patents, licenses, trademarks, and copyrights. This also comprises organizational ability, including physical systems used to send and store intellectual materials. The following factors are included here: the quality and range of information systems, the enterprise's reputation, organizational concepts, and documentation.

3. External relations capital-contact with external entities (suppliers and clients), which is of vital importance for the effectiveness of the enterprise.

Currently, there exists a growing gap between the market value and the carrying companies.

One concept of the new company's balance sheet (Dobija 2003). The overall rate allows the effectiveness of the IC of an enterprise to be measured is the relationship between value added and human capital and property damage. If the actual rate of return on tangible assets and human resources exceeds the limit, it is assumed that the assets of the company are its IC. The value of the IC will be positive if it reaches the rate of return that exceeds the risk premiums, which is taken to be 8 %. A new form of balance is preferred among other business sectors, such as engineering, consulting, and auditing. However, it is important to note the weaknesses of this form of balance sheet-no formula for the calculation of IC in an organization that adopts a threshold bonus of 8 % (Table 2.4).

There are no unequivocal means of assessing the value of IC in an enterprise. According to the literature, it is not possible to ascribe to individual employees the streams of future influences of an organization; this is because such influences typically appear as a result of the interaction between human work and tangible and intangible assets (organizational and management [Król and Ludwiczyński 2007]).

Figure 2.6 presents the total value of a company, consisting of tangible assets (tangible and financial assets recorded in the balance sheet minus liabilities) and intangible assets (the excess market value of constituents resulting from its operations).

Intellectual capital can be presented in a nonfinancial fashion by descriptions, diagrams, and this form does not indicate measured values of IC, but it is a deeper reflection of it. The measures must be tailored to suit specific businesses. The most popular measures of quality include the following:
- Danish Project of IC measurement
- Skandia Navigator
- Intangible Assets Monitor (IAM)
- IC-rating™ Model
- Value Chain Scoreboard (VCS™)
- Balanced Scorecard
- Value Explorer™ model
- Saratoga Institute Report
- Human Capital Index

The following quantitative measures of valuating IC have been indicated:
- Market value/Book value (MV/MB) indicator
- Calculated Intangible Value (CIV) indicator
- Knowledge Capital Earnings (KCE) indicator
- Value Added Intellectual Coefficient (VAIC^tm) method
- Economic Value Added
- Intangible Assets Valuation (IAV) model
- Strassmann's method
- Investor Assigned Market Value (IAMV^tm) model
- Broker's Technology

Table 2.4 Form of a balance sheet that takes IC into account

Tangible and intangible assets	Foreign capital
Intellectual assets	Equity (accounting)
	Intellectual capital

Source: (Dobija 2003)

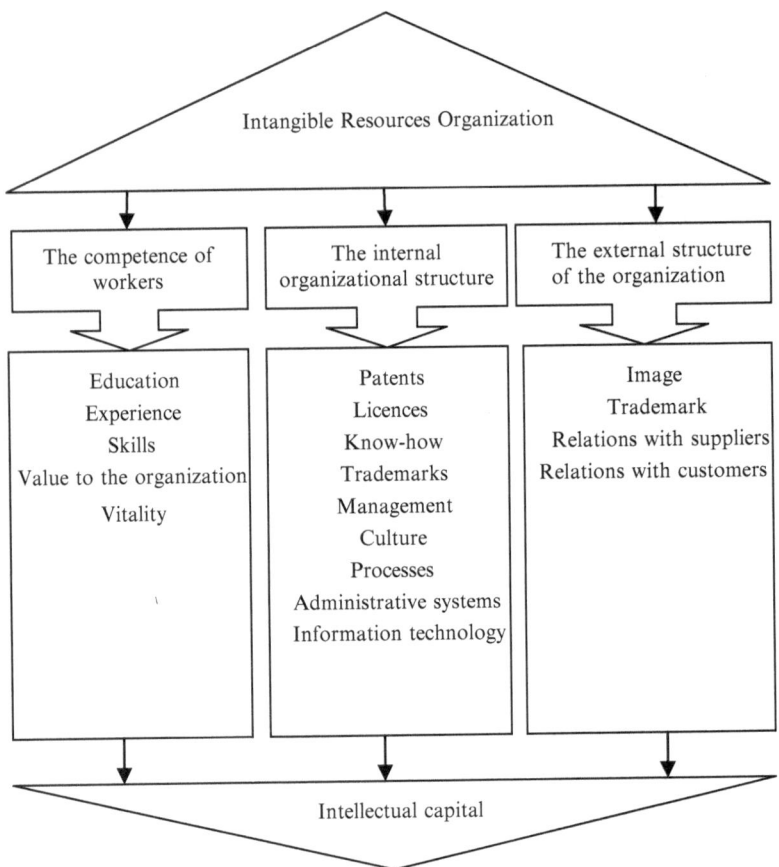

Fig. 2.6 Classification of intangible resources (Source: Sveiby 1997)

In the present study, I focus on theoretical aspects that explain the role of various categories of IC. I attempt to answer the question as to whether it is possible to speak of intangible assets as a whole, homogeneous group. Is it possible to develop a theoretical foundation and framework of guidance that would treat all categories or ingredients and components of IC equally?

2.2.3 Methods of Measuring Intellectual Capital

In both management theory and economic practice, there are many possible ways of measuring IC. Many of the suggested concepts tend to lead to ambiguous methods for assessing the value of IC in enterprises. However, the following qualitative measurements of IC have been distinguished (Mikuła 2002; Edvinsson and Malone 1997; Kasiewicz et al. 2006; Dudycz and Wrzosek 2003):

1. Danish Project of IC Measurement
   Intellectual capital is assessed based on four criteria: human resources, clients, technology, and business processes by means of indicators in three areas:
   - Statistical information (e.g., employment size and structure, training costs, number of clients, IT costs, costs of R&D activity)
   - Key internal indicators (e.g., number of training days per employee, timing when introducing a new product or service to market)
   - Indicators depicting the results (e.g., sales income, employee satisfaction).
2. Skandia Navigator
   The Skandia Navigator is based on the assumption that the true value of a company signifies its ability to generate constant value in the process of introducing a vision and strategy. The metaphor of this model is a house, and it has the following areas of focus: financial focus, customer focus, human focus, process focus, and renewal and development focus. The value of IC is the sum of the following indicators:
   1. Income from the activity of new units
   2. Investment in developing new markets (customers and programs)
   3. Investment in building the industry
   4. Investment in developing new distribution channels
   5. Investment in IT for sales, service, and support
   6. Investment in IT for administration needs
   7. Change in IT resources
   8. Investment in supporting relations with customers
   9. Investment in servicing products purchased by customers
   10. Investment in customer service training
   11. Expenditure on customers not directly connected with products
   12. Investment made to increase the quality of employee qualifications
   13. Investment in employee training
   14. Special education for employees not located in the enterprise
   15. Investment in specialist training, communication, and support for full-time employees
   16. Specialist training programs for temporary full-time employees
   17. Specialist training programs for temporary part-time employees
   18. Investment in developing alliances or joint ventures
   19. Updating systems of electronic data exchange and electronic network systems
   20. Investment in building the value of the trademark (logo and brand name)
   21. Investment in new patents and copyrights

Additionally, it is necessary to calculate the value of the indicators of IC efficiency:"I": $i = (W_{i1} + W_{i2} + \ldots + W_{i9})/9$,

where

W_{i1}—market share

W_{i2}—index of satisfied customers

W_{i3}—leadership index

W_{i4}—motivation index

W_{i5}—index of resources used for R&D goals in relation to total resources

W_{i6}—index of training hours

W_{i7}—index of achieved quality relative to planned quality

W_{i8}—employee retention

W_{i9}—administrative efficiency/incomes

3. Intangible Assets Monitor

With the IAM model (Table 2.5), it is possible to choose indicators that reflect knowledge changes and inflow into the company.

4. IC-Rating^{TM} Model

The IC-Rating^{TM} Model is based on data received from internal and external groups of 25–35 people connected with the company. The information is gathered during interviews, in which 220–240 questions are answered. The questions concern the following areas: business politics, human resources, organizational structural capital, and relational structural capital. The respondents are chosen based on their knowledge of the company and its competitors. The results of the IC-Rating^{TM} Model are presented in the form of three perspectives:

- IC efficiency
- Efforts made to renew and develop IC
- Risk of decreased effectiveness of IC

Each perspective is assessed on a scale of 0–100 or by means of a 10° letter scale, where AAA indicate the best value and D the worst (AAA, AA, A, BBB, BB, B, CCC, CC, C, and D).

5. Value Chain Scoreboard (VCS^{TM})

With this method, constructing the value of IC consists of the following stages:

1. Discovering and learning-finding new ideas for products, services, and processes. The ideas may be created in an internal innovation process in R&D and involve sharing information and aspects relating to employee experience. Ideas may also come from outside the organization.

2. Implementation—the development and assessment of the profitability of a new product or service. At the first stage, the implementation process requires a business to receive intellectual copyrights. Next, the patented product must undergo numerous examinations and tests. The final effect consists of conducting an economic assessment of the effectiveness of the investment project.

3. Commercialization—marketing activities for a newly developed product or service. Client-directed marketing activities are employed to help the company attain positive financial results.

Table 2.5 Intangible assets monitor

	Intangible assets		
	External structure	Internal structure	Individual abilities
Increase	The value of the organic increase (measures to what degree the market accepts the company's concepts and ideas)	IT investment	Tenure
		Investment in internal structures (new systems and methods)	Level of education
			Abilities Index (level of education × achievements in the profession × tenure years in the company)
			Rotation of the abilities of newly recruited employees
Modernisation/ innovativeness	Number of clients strengthening the image of the company	Number of clients strengthening the organisation	Number of clients strengthening abilities
	Sale shares for new clients	New products and services sale share	Variety of employees
	Sale shares for new markets	Number of newly introduced processes	Training and coaching costs
Efficiency	Client profitability	Participation of "support employees" (employees who make the internal structure)	Participation of professionals
	Value of sales per one client		Added value per employee
	Win/lose index (the relation of the number of offers which attracted clients to the declined offers)		Added value per professional
			Employee or professional profitability
Stability	Client satisfaction index	Values or attitudes index (employee attitudes towards work, clients and superiors)	Age of the employees
	Significant clients' share	The age of the enterprise	Tenure in the company
	Client loyalty indicator	Rotation of "support employees"	Salary discrepancy
	Age structure of the relation with clients	Number of employees with tenure shorter than 2 years	Rotation of professionals
	Regular customer share		
	Frequency of repeated orders		

The appropriate selection of indicators does not guarantee a good assessment. To adequately assess the quality of the IC, the indicators need to be interpreted.

6. Balanced Scorecard

This concept was created by Kaplan and Norton (1996). They suggested assessing activity effectiveness by analyzing four key perspectives: financial

Table 2.6 Balanced scorecard

The financial perspective	
Goals	Measurements
Survival	Cash flow
Reaching income goals	Increase of the quarterly sale
	Quarterly sale increase and operational profit of the independent budget units
Profitability	Increase in the market share
	ROE increase
	Free cash flow
The customer's perspective	
Goals	**Measurements**
New products	Percentage share of the income from the sale of new products
	Percentage share of the products covered by patent rights in the income from sales
Term deliveries (fast reaction)	On time deliveries expected by clients
Preferred supplier	Share of deliveries financed by a credit supplier
Client participation	Number of joint ventures in the area of designing new products
The perspective of internal business processes	
Goals	**Measurements**
Increase the efficiency of business processes	Value of the efficiency of each defined business processes
The perspective of innovation and the ability to learn	
Goals	**Measurements**
Technological leadership	Time necessary to prepare the next product generation
Acquiring production skills	Time necessary to reach product maturity
Concentration on profitable products	Percent of products which give 80 % or more in sales
Time of delivering a product to the market	Time necessary to introduce a new product to the market in comparison with competitors

perspective, customer's perspective, internal business processes, and innovation and learning (Table 2.6).

The Balanced Scorecard is a complex measurement and management system in an enterprise. The model is based on the assumption that innovative undertakings are equally important in terms of investment and asset management.

7. Value Explorer^{TM} Model

This model was designed by Andriessen and Tissen (2000). It is based on the core competences of enterprises, which include knowledge, skills, processes, and cultural aspects. The value of each of the core competences is calculated by means of the following variables: gross income, sustainability, potential, impact forces and capital cost:

$$Vcc = R \times \sum_{t=1}^{s} \frac{GP \times (1 + P)^t}{(1 + i)^t}$$

where
Vcc—core competence value,
R—robustness (as a percentage),
s—sustainability (in years),
GP—gross profit,
P—potential (as a percentage), and
i—capital cost.

It is assumed that the capital cost is the same for each core competence. The values of the other variables can be assessed using the scorecard. Sustainability signifies the length of time over which the enterprises can maintain a competitive advantage. Potential describes any new possibilities in the market that the company may use. Robustness indicates how deep the core competences are rooted in the company, and it is their chance of influencing the company's financial results over a longer period.

8. Saratoga Institute Report

This method is based on indicators adjusted according to an organization's area of specialization. For example, in the area of an organization's effectiveness, the following indicators are identified: income factors, cost factors, human resources, end value factors, and the profitability of investment in human resources.

9. Human Capital Index

This concept assumes that human management quality is positively correlated to the increase in the organization's market value. In research assumptions, the total return from investments by the shareholders and Q-Tobin indicator provide economic measurements for the investment in human capital.

The Q-Tobin indicator is used to interpret different phenomena in the company: outcomes of investment, relations between assets and the company's value, and relations between opportunities resulting from investment and financial policy.

The Q-Tobin indicator = market value/replacement value attached to the shares

The Q-Tobin indicator is based on the assumption that in the long term, its value will become close to 1. However, in practice, the value may differ greatly from 1; for example, some companies in the computer software industry note an indicator value higher than 7, while for other capital-consuming companies it is much lower than 1.

Additionally, the following methods of valuation of IC have been indicated:
1. Market value/Book value (MV/MB) indicator

This indicator was suggested by T. Stewart (1998). With this indicator, IC is the difference between the market value and book value of the company.

MV/BV = market value/book value

The market value is the product of the market price of a share and the number of shares. If the company is not quoted on the stock exchange, the value of shares can be determined based on valuation using a comparative method, taking into account the value of other stock exchange-listed companies. The most common method for estimating the book value is net valuation, which is the sum of the book value of all assets of the company divided by the book value of the external capital:

$$MV/BV = (1 \text{ share price} \times \text{shares number})/(\text{assets} - \text{external capital})$$

2. Calculated Intangible Value (CIV) Indicator

The initial data used in the CIV method derive from the company's financial reports over the previous 3–5 years of operation. They are also based on data from the capital market concerning the average value of the rate of return on assets (ROA). The IC value appears when the ROA for the company is higher than the ROA for the sector; otherwise, the CIV method shows a negative value. A discount rate is used if the method is estimated directly by the company or accepted as an average capital cost in the given sector.

The IC value is determined in accordance with the following stages:

Stage 1. Calculating the average profits before tax from the last 3 or 5 years of the company's activity.

Stage 2. Estimating the average value of assets for the last 3 or 5 years.

Stage 3. Dividing the average profits calculated in the first stage by the average value of assets, resulting in the average ROA.

Stage 4. Calculating the average ROA indicator for the whole sector for the last 3 or 5 years.

Stage 5. Calculating any excess by subtracting the product of the average ROA for the whole sector and the average value of the company's assets from the average profits before taxation.

Stage 6. Calculating the average taxation rate for the last 3 years, multiplying it by the excess calculated in stage 5, and then subtracting the result from the excess amount. The received amount is a premium, which falls into the category of intangible assets ("intellectual premium").

Stage 7. Calculating the current premium value by dividing the premium calculated in stage 6 by the appropriate discount rate, e.g., the capital cost for the enterprise. The calculated amount refers to the value of the intangible assets not included in the balance of the company.

The "intellectual premium" shows how much an enterprise can earn thanks to its available IC compared with an average company in the industry. The current premium value describes the value of the IC, assuming a stable economic and financial situation for the organization itself. In a comparatively simple way, the CIV method allows an estimation of the value of IC and a comparison of values among enterprises based on data from financial reports.

3. Knowledge Capital Earnings (KCE) Indicator

The KCE method is a development of the CIV method.

$$\text{Economical result} = \alpha \times \text{tangible assets} + \beta \times \text{financial assets} + \delta \\ \times \text{intangible assets}$$

The KCE method can be presented as a four-stage process:

Stage 1. Estimating the values of annual normalized profits of an enterprise. This encompasses the profits from the last 3 or 5 years and their prognosis for upcoming years. Estimating the average profits for the coming 3 to 5 years is carried out to eliminate any short-term fluctuations. A normalized profit is a net profit corrected by the value of the result from special and fortuitous events.

Stage 2. Estimating α and β, i.e., the return rate of the tangible and financial assets. Based on research and analysis of a group of global companies, Lev (2001) estimated tangible assets to be 7 % and financial assets to be 4.5 %. The return rates may be freely modified depending on the market and the condition of enterprises so that they closely reflect real economic conditions. The next step is to calculate the profit that falls on tangible and financial assets by multiplying the return rate of these assets by their value.

Stage 3. Calculating knowledge capital. The profits from tangible and financial assets received in stage 2 are subtracted from the normalized profit calculated in stage 1. Lev (2001) believed that the received difference was the profit resulting from the use of knowledge in an enterprise.

Stage 4. Calculating the total value of the knowledge capital for the whole company. To do so, the profit from intellectual knowledge calculated in stage 3 is divided by the return rate from the knowledge capital. Based on analyses of three sectors—pharmaceuticals, computer software, and biotechnology—Lev estimated this to be at the level of 10.5 %

The KCE method shows the value of IC in a company. The indicators used in the method allow an analysis of the effectiveness of IC compared with that in other competitive companies or the average for the whole sector. Knowledge capital = (normalized profit−profit from tangible and financial assets*)/discount rate of knowledge capital**

where

*—expected returns after taxation are accepted,

**—10.5 % after taxation

4. Value Added Intellectual Coefficient (VAIC^{TM}) Method

The VAIC^{TM} Method allows the value of IC to be estimated, and it can do so for companies that are not publicly traded. Furthermore, it allows the monitoring of current operational activities conducted by employees. Thus, managers can decide to what extent human capital contributes added value.

This method involves the following stages:

Stage 1. Calculating added value as the difference between the output and input of the enterprise. The results are incomes from sales of all products and services of the enterprise, whereas input constitutes all expenses except for those connected with human capital. Pulic (2000) states, "Because of the active role of the employees in creating value, expenses connected with them should not be treated as expenses."

Stage 2. Calculating the effectiveness of using traditional financial capital in creating added value. According to Pulic, three elements decide the creation of added value: the capital employed, human capital, and structural capital. The capital employed is understood as the net value of any book assets (i.e., the difference between general assets and general liabilities). The value-added capital coefficient is calculated using the relation presented in the following formula—VA/CE = VACA, where VA–value added, CE–capital employed, and VACA–value-added capital coefficient.

Stage 3. Calculating the human capital coefficient. Pulic assumes that the value of human capital may be determined as a sum of all expenses on employees—VA/HC = VAHU, where *VA*–value added, *HC*–human capital, *VAHU*–human capital coefficient.

Stage 4. Calculating the structural capital coefficient (STVA) as a relation of structural capital to value added:

SC/VA = STVA; where SC–structural capital, *VA*–value added, *STVA*, structural capital coefficient

Similar to Edvinsson, Pulic assumes that structural capital (SC) is the difference between intellectual capital and human capital, and that value of SC corresponds to value added, diminished by the value of human capital—SC = VA−HC, where SC–structural capital, *VA*–value added, *HC*–human capital.

The above formula differs from earlier effectiveness-measuring instruments since human capital and SC are in inverse proportions. We can see that if the share of human capital increases in creating value added, the share of SC decreases.

Stage 5. Summing up the indicators calculated in stages 2, 3, and 4. The received result is the value-added intellectual capital based on the enterprise's tangible and intangible assets coefficient—VAIC = VACA + VAHU + STVA, where *VAIC*–value-added intellectual capital, *VACA*–value-added capital coefficient, VAHU–human capital coefficient, and STVA–structural capital coefficient

The above method allows the measuring, monitoring and comparison of the efficiency of LED... business activity with other organizational units or other companies. The VAIC^{TM} method is objective since it is based on data taken directly from financial reports.

5. Economic Value Added

This model is based on the assumption that added value appears when the return rate of the capital is higher than the cost of capital. The method shows the sources of values from defined periods as a difference between the received capital return and its cost multiplied by the value of invested capital from each prognosis period:

$$\text{Economic value added} = \text{invested capital} \times (\text{ROIC} - \text{WACC})$$

$$\text{ROIC} = \frac{\text{net''operational''profit} - \text{corrected\_taxationl''costsl''}}{\text{investedl''capitall''}},$$

where *ROIC*–return on invested capital, *WACC*–weighted average cost of capital

6. Intangible Assets Valuation (IAV) Model

This model is based on the assumption that innovative intangible assets not only generate profit for the company, but they also develop its reputation, increase customer loyalty, and may even create an entry barrier. Innovative intangible assets and human capital constitute IC. The valuation of an enterprise operating in the market or one created through a fusion or takeover can be carried out in the following way:

VM = VTA + NPV of profits from intangible asset innovation + NPV of profits from complementary business assets + NPV of structural capital,

where *VM*–company's market value, *VTA*–accounting value of tangible assets.

7. Strassmann's Method

The formula for calculating IC according to this method is as follows: knowledge capital = value added by information/capital employed cost, while value added by information = net profit−(financial tangible assets × credit cost)

Strassman also offers a different method of calculating knowledge capital. He assumes that the company's market value added (MVA) is an effect of the owned IC, so: knowledge capital = MVA/capital cost,

where *MVA*–market value added.

8. Investor Assigned Market Value (IAMV^{TM}) Model

The model was proposed by Standfield (2002), who based it on the assumption that the difference between the market value and accounting value of an enterprise indicates the extent of its IC. In its most general form, IC is measured as the difference between market capital and accounting value. It is the most common means of measurement in the literature:

$$\text{market value} = \text{accounting value} + \text{IC materialized value}.$$

Standfield introduced two additional terms: market value, which is estimated by an investor and attainable from the enterprise's market value, and IC erosion, which is the difference between the values. It is important for managers to note that IC erosion will be limited if a company concentrates on knowledge commercialization and manages its IC.

$$\text{attainable enterprise's market value} = \text{visible capital} + (\text{IC materialized value} + \text{IC erosion})$$

9. Broker's Technology
   This IC audit provides adequate knowledge on intangible assets and makes the company more sensitive to the competitive market. This method is also resistant and successful.

Stage 1. Conduct a test in the form of 20 questions.

Stage 2. IC audit. Each element of IC is thoroughly analyzed by means of special audit questionnaires, encompassing 178 questions in total.

Stage 3. The presentation of identified IC components and their assessment using the value methods: cost, market, or income.
   As a result, a cash value for the enterprise's IC is obtained.
   Knowledge and IC have emerged as key drivers of the competitive advantage in a developed organization. So are knowledge workers the key to achieving market success? Firms should invest in their employees, especially their knowledge workers, or pay to license the patents of others. I will attempt to explain the role of the knowledge worker in relation to increasing innovation in a company in the following section.

2.2.4 Knowledge Workers or Innovative Workers?

In a company, knowledge workers need to acquire a variety of knowledge (information) about their tasks (Drucker 1988). Knowledge management in a company includes the following (Morawski 2006): (1) human resource issues: selection, development, motivation, and evaluation of knowledge workers; (2) structural and organizational issues: the selection of appropriate solutions in the level of flexibility in the structure, the degree of formalization and centralization to the effective flow of knowledge and information; (3) organizational culture issues: behavior in knowledge sharing; and (4) strategy issues: more efficient locating and acquiring knowledge from the environment.
   I will discuss here human resource issues, especially the selection of knowledge workers in a company. Knowledge workers are competent, specialized in their field, well informed, and aware of their own values and role (Morawski 2005). The literature highlights the following specializations of knowledge workers (Lord and Farrington 2006): engineers, economists, people in managerial positions in

business, planners, specialists in R&D, marketing specialists, specialists in selling, logisticians, analysts, IT professionals, people involved in the acquisition of human resources, those responsible for cooperation with other companies.

The term "knowledge worker" seems to have become common after 1973, when Peter Drucker (1973) first presented it. However, a clear definition has not yet been established. Thomas H. Davenport's definition (2005) is "knowledge workers have high degrees of expertise, education, or experience, and the primary purpose of their jobs involves the creation, distribution, or application of knowledge." Thus, describing knowledge workers as strategic-knowledge resources in a company is motivated by the following: the concept of effective management of resources in an organization (Sirmon and Hitt 2003); an enterprise's unique potential in the form of knowledge and experience (Barney 1995); and the concept of competence management (Hamel and Prahalad 1994). A strategic-knowledge resource in a company represents the knowledge, skills, and capabilities of the individuals who make up that company's workforce. Such resources are usually reflected by a person's education, experience, and specific identifiable skills (Hitt et al. 2001). Yet, how can resources—knowledge workers-be managed to create added value for enterprises?

Knowledge workers attempt to locate the appropriate knowledge from various sources, i.e., other people, the literature, and knowledge databases. Among knowledge workers, those with good knowledge can create the innovations necessary for businesses. Innovation is defined as the introduction of new, improved ways of doing things at work (Freeman and Perez 1988). In that sense, it may be appropriate to note that creating an innovative company depends on transforming as many knowledge workers as possible into innovation workers. The next section describes an innovative company and innovation workers.

I will attempt to explain that the knowledge workers in a company can enhance its innovation level. And I will show that it is possible to create a set of innovation workers as a subset of the knowledge workers in a company using the proposed Sknowinnov model (see Chap. 5).

References

Ackoff, R. L. (1974). *Redesigning the future*. New York: Wiley.

Amit, R., & Zott, C. (2001). Value creation in e-business. *Strategic Management Journal, 22*(6/7), 493–520.

Andriessen, D., & Tissen, R. (2000). *Weightless wealth: Find your real value in a future of intangibles assets*. London: Financial Times Prentice Hall.

Barney, J. B. (1995). Looking inside for competitive advantage. *Academy of Management Perspectives, 9*(4), 49–61.

Bonits, N. (1998). Intellectual capital: An exploratory study that develops measures and models. *Management Decision, 36*(2), 63.

Brooking, A. (1996). *Intellectual capital: Core asset for the third millennium* (Vol. 8, No 12–13, p. 76). London: International Thompsson Press.

Butra, J., Janowski, A., Kicki, J., Siewierski, S., & Wanielista, K. (1999). *Przedsiębiorstwo i jego otoczenie w warunkach gospodarki rynkowej (The enterprises and its environment in a market economy)*. Kraków: GSMiE PAN.

Byrne, J. A., Brandt, R., & Port, O. (1993). The virtual Corporation. *Business Week, 02*(8), 98–102.

Cascio, F. W. (2010). *Managing human resources: Productivity, quality of work life, profits* (Vol. 8). Burr Ridge: Irwin/McGraw-Hill.

Dahlman, C., & Andersson, T. (Eds.). (2000). *Korea and the knowledge-based economy*. Paris: OECD.

Davenport, T. H. (2005). *Thinking for a living, how to get better performance and results from knowledge workers*. Boston: Harvard Business School Press.

Davenport, T. H., & Prusak, L. (1998). *Working knowledge: How organizations manage what they know*. Boston: Harvard Business School Press.

Davenport, T. H., & Prusak, L. (2000). *Working knowledge: How organizations manage what they know*. Boston: Harvard Business School Press.

Davila, T., Epstein, R., & Shelton, R. (2006). *Making innovation work: How to manage it, measure it and profit from it* (pp. 262–263). Pennsylvania: Wharton Scholl Publishing.

Dobija, D. (Ed.). (2003). *Pomiar i sprawozdawczość kapitału intelektualnego przedsiębiorstwa (Measuring and reporting intellectual capital company)*. Warsaw: College of Business and Management.

Drucker, P. F. (1973). *Management: Tasks, responsibilities, practices*. New York: Harper Row.

Drucker, P. F. (1988). The coming of the new organization. *Harvard Business Review*, 01–02.

Drucker, P. F. (1994). The age of social transformation. *The Atlantic Monthly*, 11.

Dudycz, T., & Wrzosek, S. (2003). *Analiza finansowa—problemy metodyczne w ujęciu praktycznym [Financial analysis—methodological issues in practical terms]*. Wroclaw: Akademia Ekonomiczna Wrocław.

Edvinsson, L., & Malone, M. (1997). *Intellectual capital: Realizing your company's true value by finding its hidden brainpower*. New York: Harper Business.

Evans, C. (2005). *Zarządzanie wiedzą (Knowledge management)*. Warszawa: PWE.

Fazlagic, J., & Kurowski, W. (1999). Kapitał Intelektualny—przyszłość Zarządzania Przedsię – biorstwem [Intellectual capital—the future of enterprise management]. *Zeszyty Naukowe Wyższej Szkoły Bankowej w Poznaniu, 12*, 115–138.

Foray, D. (2002). The knowledge economy and society. *International Social Science Journal, 54* (171), 161–169.

Foray, D., & Lundvall, B. (1996). The knowledge-based economy: From the economics of knowledge to the learning economy. In *OECD documents: Employment and growth in the knowledge-based economy* (pp. 11–32). Paris: OECD.

Freeman, C., & Perez, C. (1988). Structural crises of adjustment, business cycles and investment behavior. In G. Dosi (Ed.), *Technical change and economic theory*. London: Pinter.

Gimeno, J. (2004). Competition within and between networks: The contingent effect of competitive embeddedness on alliance formation. *Academy of Management Journal, 47*(6), 820–842.

Grudzewski, W., & Hejduk, I. (2004). *Zarządzanie wiedzą w przedsiębiorstwach (Knowledge management in enterprises)*. Warszawa: PWN.

Gupta, J. H. D., Sharma, S. K., & Hsu, J. (2004). *An overview of knowledge management. Creating knowledge based organization*. London: Idea Grup.

Hambrick, D. C., & Cannella, A. A., Jr. (2004). CEOs who have COOs: Contingency analysis of an explored structural form. *Strategic Management Journal, 25*(10), 959–979.

Hamel, G., & Prahalad, C. (1994). *Competing for the future*. Boston: Harvard Business School Press.

Hitt, M. A., Bierman, L., Shimizu, K., & Kochhar, R. (2001). Direct and moderating effects of human capital on strategy and performance in professional service firms: A resource-based perspective. *Academy of Management Journal, 44*(1), 13–28.

Ives, W., Torrey, B., & Gordon, C. (1998). Knowledge management: An emerging discipline with a long history. *Journal of Knowledge Management, 1*(4).

Jarugowa, A., & Fijałkowska, J. (2002). *Rachunkowość i zarządzanie kapitałem intelektualnym: koncepcje I praktyka (Accounting and management of intellectual capital)*. Gdańsk: ODiDK.

Kaplan, R. S., & Norton, D. P. (1996). *The balanced scorecard: Translating strategy into action*. Boston: Harvard Business School Press.

Kasiewicz, S., Rogowski, W., & Kicińska, M. (2006). *Kapitał intelektualny [Intellectual capital]*. Krakow: Oficyna Ekonomiczna Krakow.

Kisielnicki, J. (2004). *Zarządzanie organizacją (Organization management)*. Warszawa: WSHiP.

Kotarba, M., & Kotarba, W. (2003). Model of knowledge management. *Business Economics and Organization, 8*, 14.

Kotler, P. (1994). *Marketing management:. Analysis, planning, implementation, and control*. Englewood Cliffs: Prentice Hall.

Koźmiński, A. K. (2002). How to build a knowledge-based economy? In G. W. Kolodko (Ed.), *Development of the Polish economy. Perspectives and conditions*. Warsaw: WSPiZ.

Kraciuk, J. (2005). Strategic alliances as the enterprises consolidation. *SGGW, 28*, 501.

Król, H., & Ludwiczyński, A. (2007). *Zarządzanie zasobami ludzkimi (Human resources management)*. Warszawa: PWN.

Kuznets, S. S. (1966). *Economic history. Economic development: 1945–1971*. London: Heinemann.

Lee, C., & Yang, J. (2000). Knowledge value chain. *Journal of Management Development, 19*(9), 783–794.

Leonard-Barton, D. (1995). *Wellsprings of knowledge*. Boston: Harvard Business School Press.

Lev, B. (2001). *Intangibles: Management and reporting*. Washington, DC: Brookings Institution Press.

Lindgren, R., Henfridsson, O., & Schultze, U. (2004). Design principles for competence management systems: A synthesis of an action research study. *MIS Quarterly, 28*(3), 435–472.

Lord, R. L., & Farrington, P. (2006). Age-related differences in the motivation of knowledge workers. *Engineering Management Journal, 3*, 20–26.

Lu, J. W., & Beamish, P. W. (2004). International diversification and firm performance: The s-curve hypothesis. *Academy of Management Journal, 47*(4), 598–609.

Maier, R., Haedrich, T., & Peinl, R. (2005). *Enterprises knowledge infrastructures*. Berlin/New York: Springer.

Mertins, K., Heisig, P., & Vorbeck, J. (2000). *Knowledge management: Best practices in Europe*. New York: Springer.

Mikuła, B. (2002). *Zarządzanie przedsiębiorstwem w XXI wieku. Koncepcje i metody (Enterprises management in XXI. Concepts and methods)*. Warszawa: Difin.

Morawski, M. (2005). Organizacja inteligentna [Intelligent organisation]. In *Perechuda: Zarządzanie wiedzą w przedsiębiorstwie [Knowledge management in an enterprises]*. Warszawa: PWN

Morawski, M. (2006). *Zarządzanie Wiedzą. Organizacja-System-Pracownik [Knowledge management. Organisation-system-employee]*. Wroclaw: Akademia Ekonomiczna Wrocław.

Mowshowitz, A. (1997). Virtual organization. *Communications of the ACM, 40*(9), 30–37.

Nilles, J. (1998). *Managing telework: Strategies for managing the virtual workforce*. New York: Wiley.

Nonaka, L., & Takeuchi, H. (1995). *The knowledge-creating company*. New York: Oxford University Press.

Nowell, L. T., France, R. K., Hix, D., Heath, L. S., Fox, E. A. (1996). Visualizing search results: Some alternatives to query-document similarity. In 19th annual international ACM SIGIR conference on research and development in information retrieval (SIGIR96) (pp. 67–75), Zurich. Accessed 18–22 Aug 1996.

OECD. (1996). *The knowledge-based economy*. Paris: OECD.

Picot, A., Reichwald, R., & Wigand, R. T. (1996). *Die grenzlose Unternehmung—Inforation, organisation und management*. Wiesbaden: Gabler Verlag.

Pisano, G. P., & Wheelwright, S. C. (1995). The new logic of high tech R&D. *Harvard Business Review, 73*(5).

Prahalad, C. K., & Hamel, G. (1990). The core competences of the corporation. *Harvard Business Review, 68*(3), 79–91.

Pulic, A. (2000). VAICTM—an accounting tool for IC management. *International Journal Technology Management, 20*(5/6/7/8), 702–714.

Rogers, E. M. (1995). *Diffusion of innovations.* New York: The free Press.

Schulz, Ch. (1996). Viruelle Unternehmen – Organisatorische Revolution mit Strategischer Implikation. *Management&Komputer.*

Senn, J. A. (1990). *Information systems in management.* Belmont: Wadsworth.

Sirmon, D., & Hitt, M. A. (2003). Managing resources: Linking unique resources, management and wealth creation in family firms. *Entrepreneurship Theory and Practice, 27*, 339–358.

Smith, B. L. R., & Barfield, C. E. (1996). *Technology, R&D, and the economy.* Washington, DC: The Brookings Institution.

Smith, R. A. (2002). Race, gender, and authority in the workplace: Theory and research. *Annual Review of Sociology, 28*, 509–542.

Sokołowska, A. (2005). *Managing intellectual capital in a small company.* Warsaw: The Polish Economic Society.

Stabryła, A. (Ed.). (2009). *Doskonalenie struktur organizacyjnych przedsiębiorstw w gospodarce opartej na wiedzy (Improving the organizational structure of enterprises in the knowledge-based economy).* Warszawa: Beck.

Standfield, K. (2002). *Intangible management.* Boston: Academic.

Stewart, T. A. (1998). *Intellectual capital: The new wealth of organisations.* London: Nicholas Brealey.

Sveiby, K. E. (1997). *New organizational wealth: Managing and measuring knowledge-based assets.* San Francisco: Berrett-Koehler.

Swan, J. A., Scarbrough, H., Preston, J. (1999). Knowledge management—The next fad to forget people? In Proceedings: 7th European conference on information systems, Vol. II (pp. 668–678). Copenhagen. Accessed 23–25 June 1999.

Teece, D. J. (2002). *Managing intellectual capital.* New York: Oxford University Press.

The Ministry of Economy. (2001). e-Poland—an agenda for the information society in Poland in 2001–2006

Williamson, O. E. (1975). *Markets and hierarchies.* New York: Free Press.

Zack, M. (1999). Developing a knowledge strategy. *California Management Review, 41*(3), 125–145.

Żelazny, R. (2006). Wiedza jako determinanta rozwoju gospodarczego—problemy i kontrowersje w aspekcie koncepcji gospodarki opartej na wiedzy (Knowledge as a determinant of economic development in the knowledge-based economy). In D. Kopycińska (Ed.), *Kapitał ludzki w gospodarce opartej na wiedzy (Human capital in the knowledge-based economy).* Szczecin.

Zimniewicz, K. (2000). *Współczesne koncepcje i metody zarzadzania [The modern concepts and methods of management].* Warszawa: Katedra Mikroekonomii Uniwersytetu Szczecińskiego.

Innovative Company

3

There has been a clear lack of conformity in defining "innovation" (Chandy and Tellis 2000; Green et al. 1995; Smith and Rupp 2002; Utterback and Abernathy 1975; Stryjski et al. 2008), and no consistent dimensions have been used with any of those constructs. Today, the notion of innovation is treated flexibly depending on the field of application. The concepts of innovation used in the present study require some explanation. First, innovation is thought of as an essential strategic index for a company in the process of developing and maintaining a competitive edge in the market. Second, strategic knowledge management in an innovative company should be considered a method of building strategic capacity.

It has been established that the innovative abilities of a company are dependent on the knowledge of its employees. This knowledge is strongly influenced by the quality and type of the strategic resource management in the company (Janz and Peters 2002; Engelbrecht 1997).

In this chapter, definitions of innovative companies are proposed. Furthermore, this chapter describes in detail the quantitative determinants of the direction and pace of innovation at a company level, and it defines the procedure for the strategic management of IC in an innovative company. This chapter attempts to answer the question of how to define the level of innovation in a company. It also aims to answer this question: is there a model of strategic-knowledge management that can be applied to an innovative company?

3.1 Innovativeness of Enterprises

3.1.1 Essence of Innovation

Currently, innovation is an important factor in building and maintaining a competitive advantage. Though it is understood in various different ways, the concept of innovation usually includes the following:

J. Patalas-Maliszewska, *Managing Knowledge Workers*, Management for Professionals, DOI 10.1007/978-3-642-36600-0_3, © Springer-Verlag Berlin Heidelberg 2013

- Functions describing how the volume of production varies depending on changes in input factors. Innovation is, in essence, the emergence of a new production function (Schumpeter 1939)
- Anything that is perceived as being new and independent of any objective news (Rogers 1995).
- A source of innovation in the observation of market processes and the implementation of innovation that allows a company to gain a competitive advantage in the market (Drucker 1994)
- Goods, services, or ideas that are perceived by somebody as being new (Kotler 1994)

I classify innovation according to a set of criteria:

1. The criterion of the originality of the changes:
   - Innovation, creativity (creative, original, pioneering)—of products as they first appear on the market
   - Imitating innovations (copycatting)—using an original design or making amendments to it
2. The criterion of personal and institutional feedback:
   - Combined innovation—changes as a result of a joint effort among individuals and/or institutions
   - Solo innovation—changes made by one individual in an isolated system and any subsequent rationalizing operations
3. The criterion of mechanisms to stimulate innovation:
   - Supply-side innovation—the consequence of discoveries, inventions, and ideas stimulated by scientific developments
   - Demand innovation—driven by the needs of a market
4. The criterion of internal innovation:
   - Product innovation (for products and services)—the improvement to an existing product manufactured by a company or manufacturing a new, improved product. The new product is made up of different materials to the earlier product
   - Product innovation may be based on new technologies combined with existing technologies and employed in new applications
   - Process innovation—changes involving the method of product manufacture and transporting products to markets. These changes may include the introduction of new equipment or the manner of production
   - Organizational innovation—a more effective way of managing the organization and its products, research efforts, and services
   - Marketing innovation—development of new forms of promotion of products or services

By definition, an innovation index (function) is a concise quantitative indicator of the innovative capability of institutions, researchers, businesses, and territories in selected areas of research (Aspen Institute 2007). Put another way, it is a tool to measure, monitor, and promote the progress of innovation performance. The index (function) may also serve as a quantitative benchmark of capability, highlighting the resource commitments and policy choices that mostly affect long-term innovative output (Porter and Stern 1999; Porter 1998). Many studies (e.g., studies of innovation index by the IMD, WEF, OSLO Manual, Commission of the European Communities, INSEAD) take into account various aspects of innovation in a company.

The innovation potential of a company is essentially the ability to implement innovation effectively—new products, technology, organizational methods, and marketing innovation (Poznańska 1998). There are two types of innovation potential: internal, which includes the company resources; and external, which includes resources from outside the company but which are available to the company.

The introduction of innovation in a company allows for extension of its product market or service range and for adjusting what it offers to meet the needs of its customers. Nevertheless, the range and speed of innovation in small and medium-sized enterprises is restricted compared with those of large enterprises, which typically have their own R&D infrastructure and the financial means to allow extensive research.

Some of the factors of a structure that facilitate innovation are as follows:
- A flat organization structure
- A low level of formality of operation
- Decentralization, the delegation of responsibilities
- A teamwork system
- Customer-oriented activities
- A developed informal structure (the number of informal relationships)
- Efficient two-way information flow

Actions that lead to the development of a business, its knowledge integration, and innovation are a significant factor in the competitive edge of that business (Pisano and Wheelwright 1995; Patalas and Kłos 2007).

Thus, it can be summarized that the innovativeness of enterprises is essentially the ability and motivation to follow business and commercial exploitation of R&D.

3.1.2   External and Internal Determinants of an Innovative Company

The area of development of innovative companies is an important element in the level of innovation and business competitiveness of a country. It is necessary to create lasting links between companies and R&D institutions so that the former have continued access to innovative knowledge.

The success of a company lies in its capacity to create or implement innovations in a given time period. Creating innovation requires cooperation and mutually complementary competences that cannot be conducted independently or separately. Innovation is always associated with the transfer of knowledge and technology to the enterprise. Developing an increased interest in innovation requires the development of a specific infrastructure and building a pro-innovation culture, for example, through the establishment of R&D centers.

A company has to search for adaptations of innovative solutions so as to adjust to changes in the environment and to obtain or maintain a market advantage. For a small firm, it is clearly difficult for it to commit all its resources to building or adapting innovative solutions (Child and Faulkner 1998; Dyer and Singh 1998). One solution that allows companies to create or implement innovations would appear to be in formally organized networks of business cooperation with R&D efforts. This can have the effect of combining the resources of many collaborating companies in creating and disseminating innovative solutions; it also allows links to be developed such that a company can focus on its key skills (competences).

Innovative companies "should now become the main force of any creative organization, permanently inscribed in its management and culture" (Pomykalski 2001). Thus, I can state that an innovative company has continuous access to information from its surroundings and can create or acquire and implement innovation.

Insufficient internal capacity to create business innovation encourages company management to seek innovation in an environment of financial and technical knowledge. Developing a capacity to absorb and use knowledge generated outside the company is becoming a key factor in a company's development. Innovative companies should have a management system that is organized in accordance with the principles of systematic innovation, which requires tracking all sources of innovation (Drucker 1994; Smith and Barfield 1996; Steinmann and Schreyoegg 2000; Sveiby 1997; Swan et al. 1999; Hitt et al. 1997). In the following section, I define the external determinants of an innovative company.

3.1.2.1 Training Center

This is a non-profit advisory body of information and training that works to promote entrepreneurship and self-employment; it improves the competitiveness of small and medium-sized enterprises. Training centers participate in any initiatives that are designed to expand the economic potential and improve the quality of life of a community. The objectives of these centers are integrally related to the needs and requirements of local labor markets and new technologies.

3.1.2.2 Technology-Transfer Center

These centers constitute a mixed group of organizational non-profit advisory bodies and training and support programs for implementing IT transfer and commercialization and all accompanying tasks. Being at the interface of science and business (hence frequently known as "bridges"), technology-transfer centers absorb new technologies by working with small and medium-sized companies. The basic operations of the centers include promoting the potential for science and innovation in the region, creating databases, and development networks between science and the economy. They also deal with the development of pre-investment studies; these include identifying the benefits of new products and technologies and comparing them with existing ones. In addition, these centers assess potential markets and estimate the costs of production, distribution, and necessary investment. Further, they identify the needs and opportunities for innovative individual operators (technological audit) so as to popularize, promote, and develop technological entrepreneurship.

3.1.2.3 Technology Incubator

Technology incubators are organized economic complexes that involve a wide group of both isolated and well-located centers that have facilities for offering support services to small and medium-sized companies. The operations of these complexes are targeted at supporting the development of newly established companies and optimizing the conditions for technology transfer and commercialization through the following: providing adequate space for the needs of businesses; business support services, such as economic consultancy, financial support, legal support, patents, and organizational and technological help; assistance in raising funds; creating a proper climate for the establishment and implementation of innovative projects and synergistic effects; contact with scientific institutions and evaluating innovative projects.

3.1.2.4 Science and Technology Park

Science and technology parks chiefly deal with activities related to the following:
- Searching for new solutions in technology and fostering innovative companies
- Providing cooperation among numerous entities, such as educational centers, R&D centers, business entities, counseling organizations, and financial and training institutions
- Supporting technology transfer

3.1.2.5 Personnel Transfer Center

These centers are dedicated to supporting the mediation of qualified personnel in businesses to produce an improvement in business performance.

3.1.2.6 Regional Contact Points

In the case of Europe, these promote possibilities for accessing EU funding.

Such defined activities help to increase business interest in investing in scientific R&D and developing a better flow of research results between laboratories and industry. Also, it can enhance the growth and improve the competitiveness of the local region through the expansion of facilities to encourage the development of research, innovation, and technology.

However, getting companies to become interested in gaining the new business solutions (in the form of, among other areas, implementing innovation, technology transfers, and acquiring industrial property rights) that are necessary for their development is a major challenge. This challenge is so great that it requires the intervention of the state. The activities of R&D centers help increase business interest by encouraging investment in research work and developing a better flow of research results between R&D institutions and interested enterprises. R&D institutions are needed for the following (Fig. 3.1):
- Improvement of the business environment for business creation in the form of technical infrastructure and management consulting

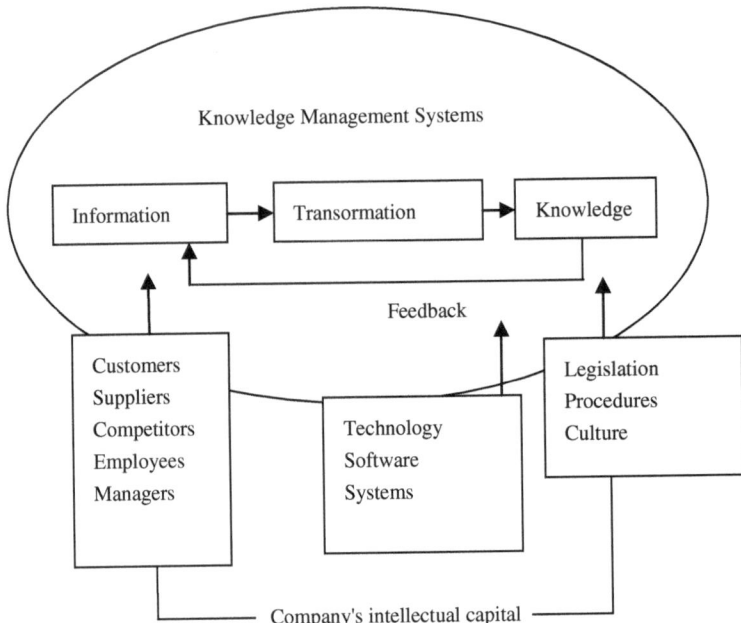

Fig. 3.1 Knowledge-management systems-a schematic picture

- Furthering cooperation and effective information flow between R&D and the business operations in a region
- Cost-effective commercialization of research (Fig. 2.3)

A company operates in an uncertain environment, and therefore when its actions lead to the creation or acquisition of innovation, those actions must be based on the company's characteristics. I will now present the uncertain environment that operates in an innovative company.

3.1.2.7 Economic Environment for R&D Activities

A strategic analysis of the economic environment in R&D consists of determining the values of the following parameters characterized by the macroeconomic situation of a country:

- GDP
- Domestic demand
- Gross fixed capital formation
- Investment rate
- Inflation
- Foreign direct investment
- Number of newly registered businesses in the country
- Number of active businesses
- Profitability of gross and net business
- First-degree financial liquidity of companies

- Liquidity of second-stage firms
- Sources of investment for companies
- Domestic loans, own funds, funds from foreign aid, from the EU and the budget
  The development potential of a company is understood as being the level of investment activity and source of investment financing. In creating or acquiring an innovative company, it is necessary to conduct an analysis of the strategic economic environment according to the indicators listed above, taking into account the forecast values for those parameters and assessing the potential trend of their changes. Such data can be obtained from reports produced by the central statistical office of a country. If the values of economic growth, domestic demand, gross fixed capital formation, and foreign investment have an upward trend, it may be assumed that the economic environment is favorable for a company. If a company wishes to be innovative, it should seize such opportunities so as to be ahead of its innovative competitors. This underlines the importance of accurate data on the profitability of gross and net turnover of companies and their liquidity and information about the source of investment financing.

3.1.2.8 Regulatory Environment for R&D Activities

A decisive role in shaping innovative companies is played by state policies and any related innovation policies. State policies can promote a country's innovation efforts by encouraging competition and innovation in the form of private sector expenditure on R&D and improving the management of public funds allocated to R&D activities.

The following examples are laws that were introduced in Poland that aimed to improve the level of business innovation:

- The Act of 29 July, 2005 on certain forms of support for innovation activities
- The Act of 8 October, 2004 on the principles of financing science
- The Act of 25 July, 1985 on R&D

3.1.2.9 Social Environment for R&D Activities

The individual worker plays an extremely important role in building a strategy for a company. An organization's competitive advantage does not arise from the possession of technology, but the possession of knowledge. A company's employees represent the company's growth potential. The appropriate management of knowledge in an organization at the strategic level can provide a competitive advantage in the market. The integration of knowledge is essential in this process, and it also helps in establishing a project team within a company. "New employees are always welcome when their characters interact well with those of other team members" (Belbin 2007). The features of all team members should be adjusted such that there are no conflicts and that the use of time is as efficient as possible while meeting the required work quality levels. The team is a group of people working together to achieve its target. Following on from this concept, is it possible to distinguish factors that limit the functioning of project teams, including:

- Limited number of specialists from different fields
- Skilled workers unable to be assigned work on two parallel projects

- The total time required exceeds 100 h per week
- People with different personality traits may be unable to work together without some form of conflict arising
  The following can be identified as key parameters in the social environment:
- Demographic situation in the country (including international migration)
- Average level of employment in the enterprise sector
- Age structure of unemployed people
- Dynamics of changes in companies
- Number of employees with higher education in the company
- Number of employees with experience in international collaboration

For a company to be innovative, it must include, among other factors, the following in its social environment: the availability of workers with higher education and their appropriate professional experience; the availability of managerial staff with experience in international collaboration. The acquisition of appropriate staff will allow a company to establish contact with R&D organizations and become internationally competitive.

3.1.2.10 Technological Environment for R&D Activities

An analysis of the technological environment should be carried out to obtain information about new technological solutions in the country, centers that offer technological advice, quality standards for products and production processes, and the cost of purchasing and implementing new technologies. With this in mind, the following indicators can be highlighted:

- Value of investments in new technologies
- Value of investments in know-how
- Value of investments in licenses
- Value of investments in fixed assets (machinery and equipment)
- Value of investments in transportation
- High-end value of investment in technology
- Value of investing in the company's own R&D
- Amount invested in purchasing R&D

3.1.2.11 International Environment for R&D Activities

Increasing international competition is forcing the growth of interest in innovative business solutions.

If changes in domestic or foreign trade are unfavorable, this may result in fewer opportunities for a firm to acquire or transfer innovation on the international market.

However, there are also internal factors for an innovative company:

- Personality factors that arise from the business (organizational skills, creativity, desire to stand out, openness to innovation)
- Factors associated with the entrepreneurial experience
- Factors related to company personnel
- Factors related to the close working environment

- Factors arising from the company's location (e.g., the possibility of contact with R&D enterprises)
- Company results (sales growth, earnings, liquidity) and any legal considerations relating to the company

To become innovative, enterprises should regularly carry out analyses of the strategic environment. The results of such work will enable a company to obtain a competitive advantage through knowledge of important trends and determinants in the market. The creation and practical introduction of product, technology, and organizational innovation requires exploitation of the company's relevant technical, scientific and market innovation. With regard to internal information sources for innovation, I would include the following factors:

- Owner of the information and knowledge
- Information- and knowledge-management board
- The company's own research activities
- Marketing of information services

For a company, gaining access to the latest knowledge can provide a chance to acquire a competitive advantage over larger enterprises, which can lead to the expansion of R&D on a greater scale. IT can significantly contribute to the increasing innovation of an enterprise.

Along with the development of IT, new solutions have been developed for an Enterprise Resource Planning system—ERP systems. Increasingly, manufacturers of these systems observe the needs of the market and adjust specific areas of the functionality of their ERP systems to meet the needs of other companies. In addition, the basic modules in the ERP system are based on an integrated database: shopping modules, manufacturing, materials management, sales, cost accounting, fixed assets, financial modules, and accounting. It is now possible to find the following. Supply chain management (SCM) in a company can optimize long-term benefits (Sarkis and Gunasekaran 2003). Internet technology can support ERP systems as follows: business to business (B2B) involves general relationships between businesses, auto search and analysis of information services, and automated transactions; business to customer (B2C) is generally the relationship between the firm and the client in the retail market; automatic retrieval and analysis of information services; and automated transactions (Sarkis and Gunasekaran 2003). There are also enterprise portals, customer relationship management (CRM)—a business strategy that relies on building relationships and managing customers to optimize long-term benefits (Sarkis and Gunasekaran 2003)), and even workflow management. Each of the individual modules of the system meets certain areas of the enterprise support functions (Wei and Wang 2004).

Implementation of the ERP system is a strategic decision by a company, and it can determine the effects of resource use and management efficiency. The competitiveness and innovation of a company is considered in terms of financial aspects, such as volume profits, turnover, and making investments; however, it is also thought of in its ability to respond quickly to market needs, offer more efficient customer service, reduce the time needed for the design and implementation of new products, and the ability to manage information. The ability to meet information

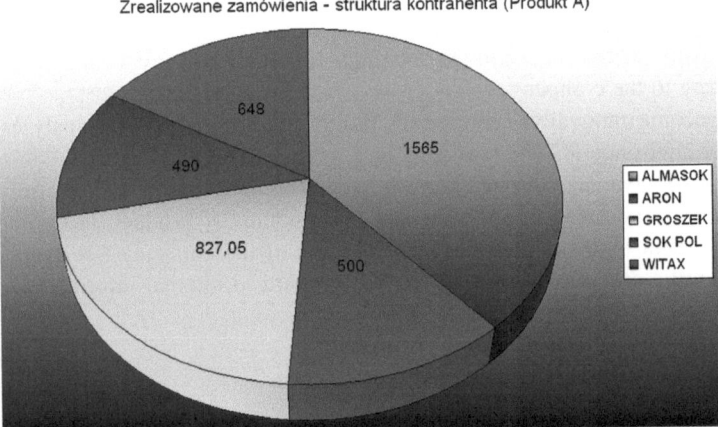

Fig. 3.2 Example of a report using business intelligence—contract executed: the contractor structure

needs creates an opportunity to provide all the internal and external users in the company with all necessary information and appropriate updates. The need to provide the necessary information for achieving the company's economic goals determines the decision to implement an integrated management system.

There is a strong correlation between a company's competitive position in the market and the company's activities, such as investments (including new technologies and human capital), exports, and the use of external financing.

A short discussion is presented here about the knowledge-management system, which allows a company to be innovative. Knowledge management in enterprises requires an appropriate system (Fig. 3.2). Such a system allows the following:

- Acquiring knowledge about information
- Preventing any loss of knowledge
- Preserving knowledge
- Sharing knowledge
- Streamlining the process of new product introduction
- Accelerating product development cycles
- Raising the level of innovation

Information is inputted to knowledge-management systems (Hitt et al. 2004; Hays and Kearney 2001; Gupta et al. 2004; Farazmand 2003, 2004; Drucker 1994; Haas-Edersheim 2007; Hill and Jones 2000; Kogut and Zander 1992). Knowledge management plays a significant role in the implementation of a corporate strategy, increasing the speed of the decision-making process. The success of an enterprise will depend on the development level of techniques and methods used for communicating information and transforming it into knowledge. One solution that allows the capture, analysis, and processing of information is business intelligence.

Business intelligence (Chen and Liang 2000) consists of the following:

- Information analyzed to the point where it is sufficient for decision making

- A tool for informing company officials
- A means of analyzing and assessing the market situation
- A continuous process that covers the entire enterprise
- A way of thinking
- A philosophy

A business intelligence system will operate effectively if it is based on modern IT. As a result, the management of information flow, the generation of summary reports, the making of presentations, and data visualization can all be performed automatically. IT can be regarded as a strategic company resource if information links and analytical information are generated by transactional systems as a company develops (IT becomes a tactical tool if companies are organized in terms of ERP, CRM, and SCM). An example of a business intelligence solution for companies is the Comarch CDN XL Business Intelligence tool (BI) (http://www.comarch.pl/erp/oferta/produkty/comarch-cdn-xl/funkcjonalnosc/raportowanie#bi), which is a complete system for managing all the processes within a company. This system also supports reporting from more than just the corporate database: it can enable the consolidation of information relating to the various actors, and it does not require work or the use of costly, time-consuming external studies. Furthermore, this system easily allows the creation of a summary analysis of aggregate data from the sales of many vendors and allowing separate analyses of each party. Business intelligence allows reports to be viewed anywhere at any time. It includes the following features:

- The ability to distribute reports to a recipient's e-mail address—subscription
- Access to reports in a Web browser—e-bi
- The ability to view reports on a mobile device—Comarch mobile manager
  Sample reports appear in Figs. 3.2, 3.3, and 3.4.

Building human resource capacity in a company involves developing employees with the desired characteristics and skills. Such employees can lead to the creation of increased business performance (value added) and to the attainment of a competitive advantage.

3.2   Model of an Innovative Company

3.2.1   Organizational Structure of Knowledge-Oriented Companies

A knowledge-oriented company brings together the potential competence of relationships and useful information. These determine the suitability of current requirements and processes and future opportunities generated by the business environment (Koźmiński 2002). The development trends of knowledge-oriented companies are as follows (Grudzewski and Hejduk 2004; Mikuła et al. 2002; Perechuda 2005; Garvin 2006; Pedler et al. 1996; Senge 1998; Baldridge et al. 2004):

- Focusing attention on managing intangible values of the organization (creating IC across the organization) as a means of building a market advantage;

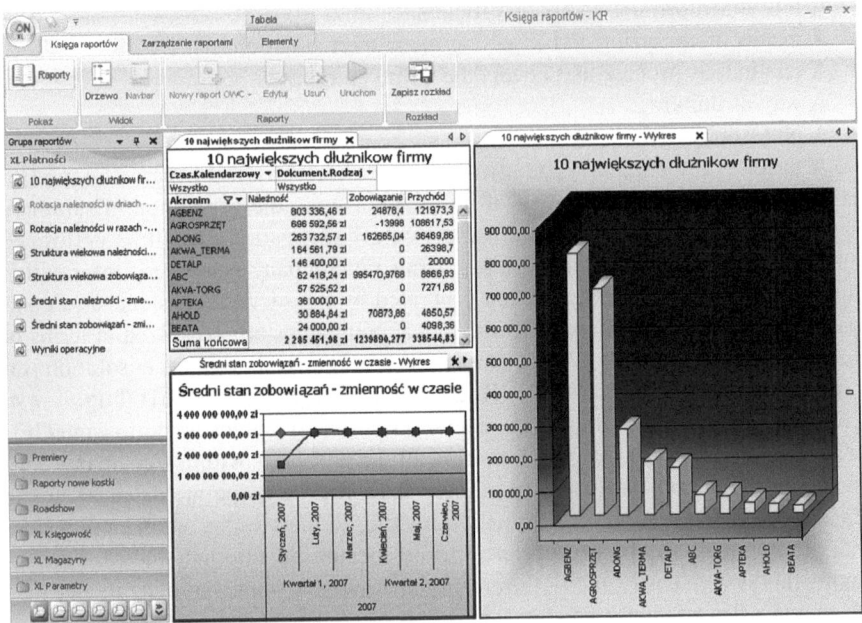

Fig. 3.3 Example of a report using business intelligence

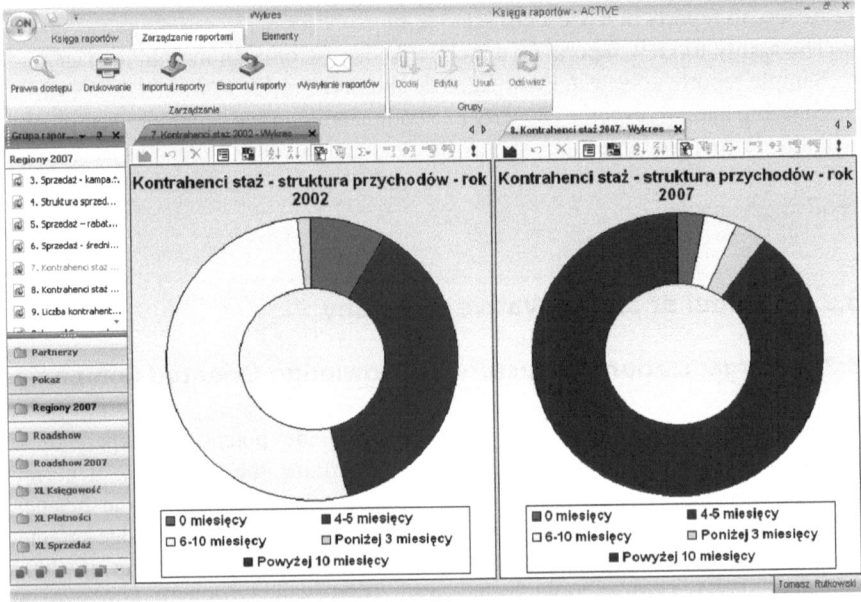

Fig. 3.4 Example of a report using business intelligence

knowledge is regarded as an essential factor in manufacturing and replaces traditional sources of growth by initiating and leading the value-added potential within other intangible and tangible resources

- Management is focused on creative, intellectual impulses that link opportunities with the competence of employees and organizations, thereby allowing for increasingly complex control and direction
- Management is internally consistent; the boundaries between functional areas are removed by the positive feedback resulting from the continuous exchange of information, which is built on the basis of comprehensive knowledge about customers, suppliers, competitors, technologies, and products
- Focusing on creating favorable conditions for cooperation
- The knowledge-management system creates a consistent, harmonized whole with other key elements of management—strategy, structure, procedures, and organizational culture
- Cooperation and collaboration with first-class professionals (knowledge workers), possessing the necessary responsibilities to achieve a competitive position for the organization
- Employees are expected to adopt attitudes and behavior that are consistent with intellectual commitment; in turn, a knowledge-oriented company is aimed at promoting ingenuity and a subjective approach among employees, thereby encouraging self-organization
- A focus on the subjectivity of competent workers is ultimately achieved by creating a community culture of professionals, which affirms dialogue, partnership, trust, and responsibility
- Knowledge is used with the client, which provides value based on professionalism and partnership in relations

Learning and knowledge management in a company have become fundamental issues of theory and practice (Barkema and Vermeulen 1998; Chakravarthy et al. 2003). Interest in organizational learning has grown with the decline of some well-established firms, the diminishing competitive power of many companies in a burgeoning world market, and the need for organizational renewal and transformation. Managers in many organizations are convinced of the importance of improving learning within their organizations. This growth in awareness has raised many questions. What are the restrictions on knowledge oriented-companies? How can organizations improve their knowledge?

To improve knowledge in an organization, it is necessary to establish a knowledge-based structure (Skyrne 1999; Stabryła 1991; Stacey 1992). A traditional hierarchical management structure is presented in Fig. 3.5.

A knowledge-based organizational structure appears in Fig. 3.6. The knowledge organization in Fig. 3.6 consists of knowledge groups that are made up of knowledge teams; these in turn comprise knowledge workers, who are selected for their tacit knowledge and skills. Ideally, the knowledge workers on any knowledge team come from different organizational (and educational) backgrounds and bring a diversity of tacit knowledge and skills to the team. The organic structure will facilitate the development of a "knowledge culture" within an organization: first,

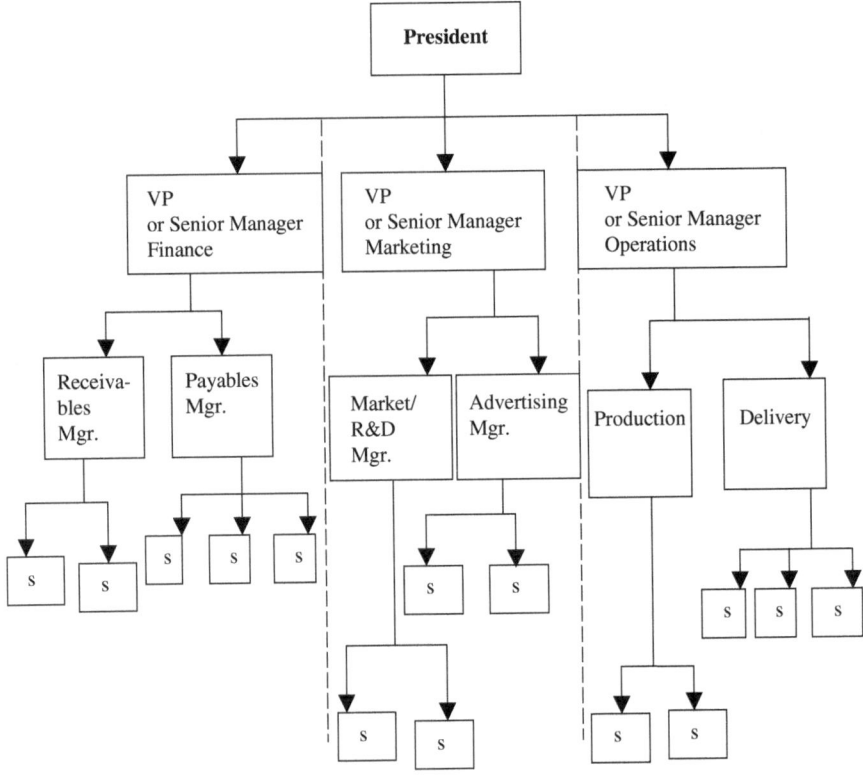

s-staff

Fig. 3.5 Traditional management hierarchy in an organization (s-staff) (Source: Walczak 2005)

by supporting the decision making of knowledge workers through collaboration in knowledge teams (real or virtual); second, by facilitating the exchange of tacit knowledge through interaction in knowledge teams with other knowledge workers (Walczak 2005).

In the literature are distinguished inter alia the following structural models for knowledge oriented-companies: an innovative company (Jasiński 1992); a virtual company (Perechuda 1997); a process-oriented company (Romanowska and Trocki 2004); a fractal company and a learning company (Senge et al. 1999). Because of the subject matter of this paper, a detailed description will be reserved for the innovative company.

3.2.1.1 Virtual Company: As Defined in Sect. 2.2.1

In this model, assets resources play the most important role (Perechuda 1997). This model is characterized by its working environment—the implementation of tasks is carried out by employees at their homes using computers and related tools.

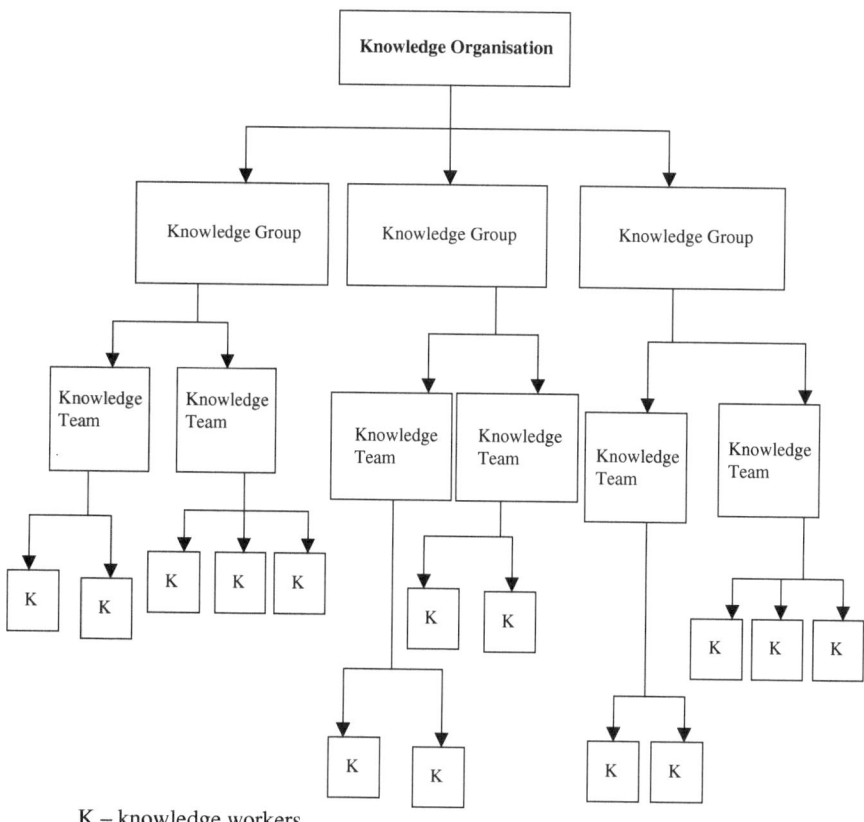

K – knowledge workers

Fig. 3.6 Elements of the hierarchy of a knowledge organization (K—knowledge workers) (Source: Walczak 2005)

3.2.1.2 Process-Oriented Company

The organization structure is flat (Romanowska and Trocki 2004). The work is conducted by multi-teams, which are responsible for implementing processes.

3.2.1.3 Fractal Company

The organization structure is flat. The work is carried out by autonomous teams.

3.2.1.4 Learning Company

Managers in many organizations are convinced of the importance of improving learning in their organizations. The basic characteristics of a learning organization and creating knowledge are as follows:

- The use of knowledge as a basic resource
- Treating knowledge as a source of value for all stakeholders
- Flexibility in organizational structure
- Future orientation

- Increased opportunities for self-organization
- Use of IT
- Use of modern communications, such as the Internet, Extranet, Intranet
- An organizational culture that facilitates the flow of innovations (Maier 2002; Pedler et al. 1996)

Thus, learning organizations are characterized as follows. "Organizations where people continually expand their capacity to create the results they truly desire, where new and expansive patterns of thinking are nurtured, where collective aspiration is set free, and where people are continually learning to see the whole together." (Senge et al. 1999; Vermuelen and Barkema 2001).

> A vision of what might be possible. It (the learning organization) is not brought about simply by training individuals; it can only happen as a result of learning at the whole organization level. A Learning Company is an organization that facilitates the learning of all its members and continuously transforms itself. (Pedler et al. 1996)

Learning organizations are "characterized by total employee involvement in a process of collaboratively conducted, collectively accountable change directed towards shared values or principles" (Watkins and Marsick 1992).

3.2.1.5 Innovative Company

Innovation capability refers to the ability to make major improvements and modifications to existing technologies and to create new technologies (Furman et al. 2002; Romjin and Albaladejo 2000; INSEAD 2007). Within a country, an innovation index could function as a measure to ascertain the degree to which conditions in clusters contribute to the national innovative capability.

The International Institute for Management Development (IMD) and the World Economic Forum (WEF) are two major global organizations that focus on developing science, technology, and innovation capability indexes. The IMD's main factors for measuring the innovative capability of nations include the following:

- Economic performance—the macroeconomic evaluation of the domestic economy, international trade, international investment, employment rates, and prices
- Government efficiency—the extent to which government policies are conducive to competitiveness, including public finance, fiscal policies, institutional frameworks, business legislation, and societal frameworks
- Business efficiency—the extent to which the national environment encourages enterprises to perform in an innovative, profitable, and responsible manner; factors here include productivity and efficiency, the labor market, finance and management practices, and attitudes and values
- Infrastructure—the extent to which basic, technological, scientific, and human resources meet the needs of businesses; factors here include basic infrastructure, technological infrastructure, scientific infrastructure, health care, the environment, and education (The IMD World Competitive Year Book 2008)
  Competitiveness factors defined by the WEF are as follows:
- Basic requirements—institutions, infrastructure, the macro-economy, health care, and elementary education

- Efficiency enhancers—higher education and training, market efficiency, and technological readiness
- Innovation and sophistication—business sophistication and innovation (The Global Competitiveness Report 2008–2009, World Economic Forum (WEF))

Many studies (e.g., the studies on innovation indexes by the IMD, WEF, OSLO Manual, the Commission of the European Communities, INSEAD) provide different factors regarding innovative capability according to their international perspective. However, an innovation index reflects a nation's overall capability to innovate (from generating new ideas to the design, development, and diffusion of innovations). The above studies examine various levels of innovation and measuring them in a company.

An analysis of an innovative company is based on five dimensions: (1) organization innovation capability; (2) process innovation capability; (3) service innovation capability; (4) product innovation capability; and (5) marketing innovation capability. The dimensions of the innovation capability index and its description can be summarized as follows:

- Organization innovation capability—this indicates the ability of a business to accept new ideas and provide new knowledge to employees. The index can indicate an ability to create innovations in various sectors and the acceptance of changes at all levels.
- Process innovation capability—this indicates the ability of a business to adjust the production process at all levels, including inventory distribution, logistics, and any ancillary supporting activities of the accounting, purchasing, and finance departments.
- Service innovation capability—this indicates the ability of a business to provide new knowledge or technologies in developing a new service that results in a significant improvement to the production or delivery of goods or services.
- Product innovation capability—this indicates the ability of a business to produce new knowledge or technology in developing product innovations, thereby increasing revenue at all levels.
- Marketing innovation capability—this indicates the ability of a business to implement a technologically new or improved product or process for its operating market (Research Report of Thailand Innovation Capability Index (National Innovation Agency and King Mongkut's University of Technology Thonburi)—year).

It has therefore been clearly established that the innovative abilities of a company are dependent on the knowledge of its employees. A company is innovative because of its organizational capacity and through its application of IC.

Knowledge within a company is strongly influenced by the quality and type of its employees' formal education (Janz and Peters 2002; Teixeira and Fortuna 2006; Engelbrecht 1997). Knowledge plays a special role in the innovation process. In relation to other innovation factors, knowledge is as follows:

- Complete (it determines the ability to create, adapt, and implement innovation; it has both domestic and foreign sources)
- Non-substitutional (in marketing or organizational innovations)

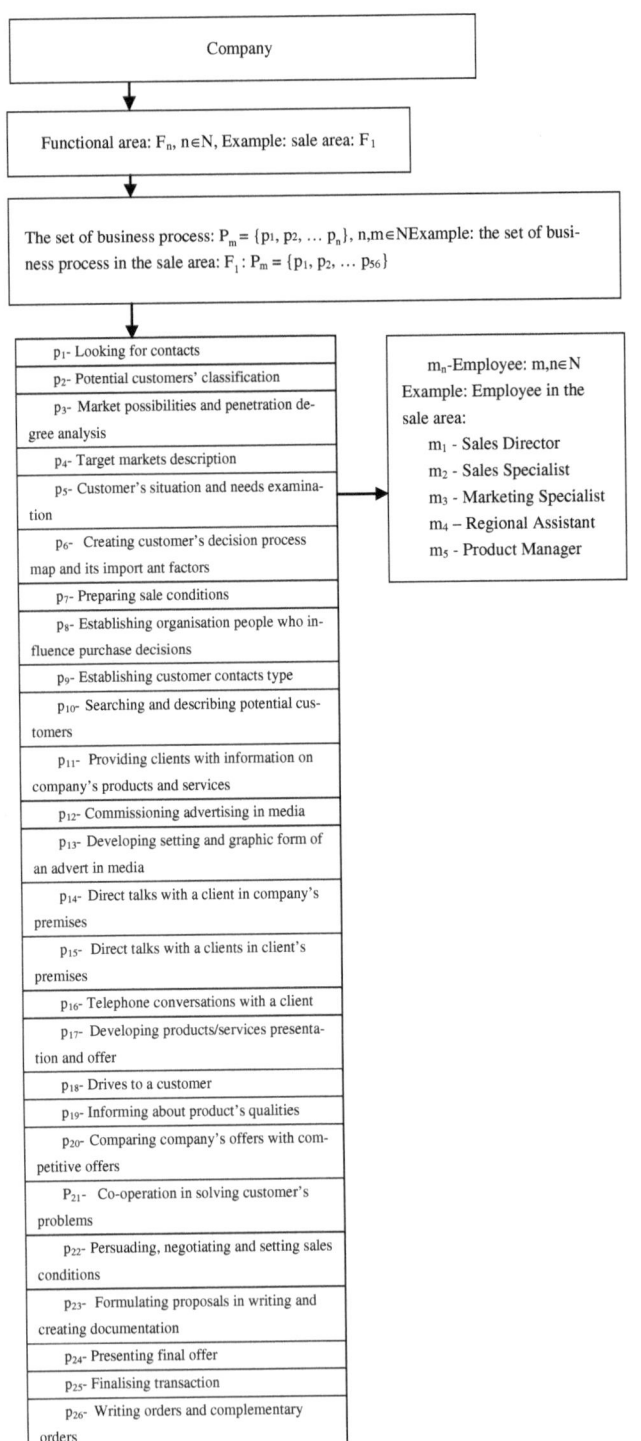

Fig. 3.7 (continued)

p$_{27}$- Registering order for a supplier
p$_{28}$- Purchase registering
p$_{29}$- Sales and delivery registration
p$_{30}$- Invoicing
p$_{31}$- Registering returns and value corrections of commercial documents
p$_{32}$- Credit, invoice and payment collection problem solving
p$_{33}$- Claims and collecting products from customers
p$_{34}$- Stocktaking, stock control
p$_{35}$- Stock monitoring
p$_{36}$- Developing marketing programmes
p$_{37}$- Conducting market analysis for the needs of a customer
p$_{38}$- Presenting new products and technologies
p$_{39}$- Production problems solving
p$_{40}$- Meeting participation
p$_{41}$- Administrative work
p$_{42}$- Trainings participation
p$_{43}$- Supervision of completing the sales schedule
p$_{44}$- Quantity and quality claims servicing
p$_{45}$- Gathering data in a database on clients, potential clients, markets.
p$_{46}$- Delivery notification
p$_{47}$- Sales prognosis
p$_{48}$- Customers segmentation
p$_{49}$- Customer contact centres
p$_{50}$- Suppliers bidding
p$_{51}$- Settling up Sales representatives
p$_{52}$- Sales representatives' router planning
p$_{53}$- Planning types and elements of sales representatives' visits
p$_{54}$- Creating sales representatives' tasks
p$_{55}$- Reporting company's products and competitive products at customer's premises.
p$_{56}$- Creating sales plans for sales regions

Fig. 3.7 Model of knowledge worker-oriented company with an example of business processes in sales

- Substitutional (after the introduction of topical innovation, a less qualified labor force is replaced by a better-qualified one)
  Thus, an innovation-oriented company has the following features:
- It conducts large-scale R&D (or purchases new technologies)
- It has the ability to obtain and generate innovation
- It is flexible toward the changing market
- It systematically implements new solutions

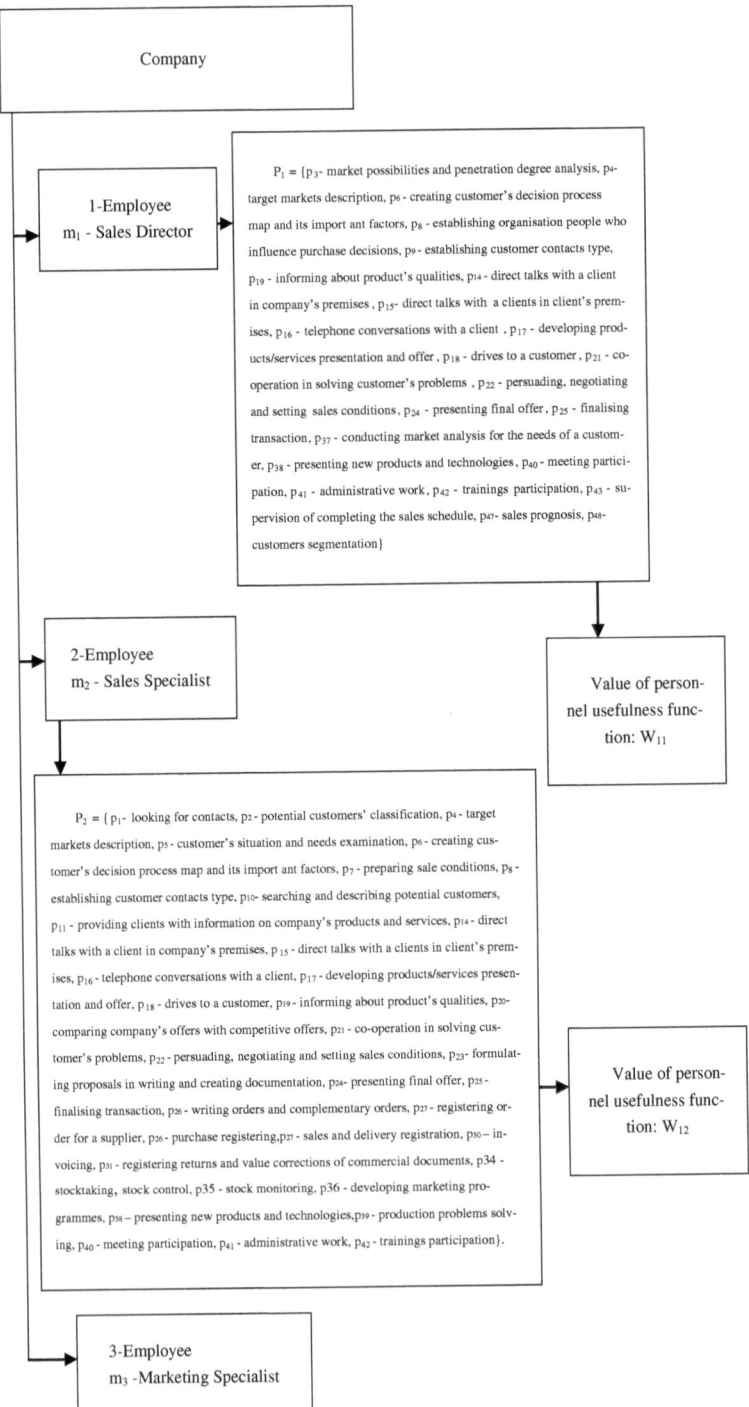

Fig. 3.8 (continued)

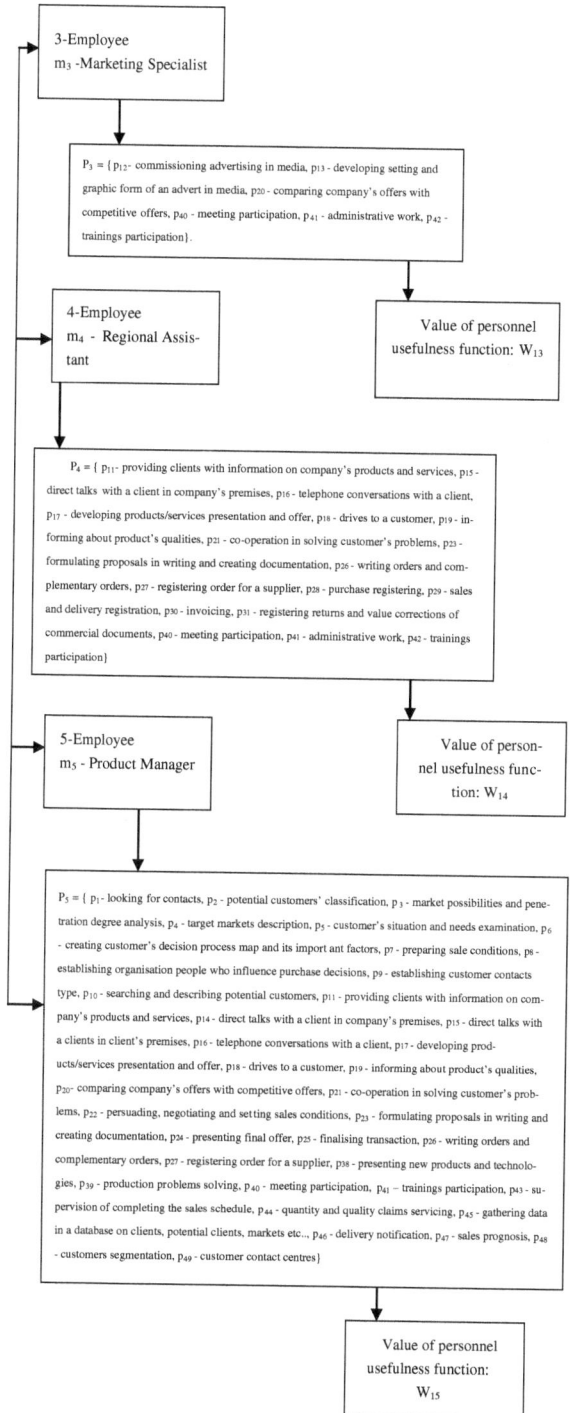

Fig. 3.8 Model of knowledge worker-oriented company—example in the sales area

- It has a wide share of new products within its whole product range
- It constantly introduces innovation to the market (Jasiński 1992).

3.2.2 Model of Knowledge Worker-Oriented Company

I distinguish the value of knowledge workers as being specialists in selling, as follows: m1, sales director; m2, sales specialist; m3, marketing specialist; m4, regional assistant; and m5, product manager. I have done this in terms of their so-called personnel usefulness function. Figure 3.8 presents a model of a knowledge worker-oriented company with the knowledge workers as specialists in selling.

The model includes business processes, employees (description of workplaces), and the so-called personnel usefulness function (see Chap. 4). The business processes in each functional area in the company comprise employee activities. The personnel usefulness function is defined for each employee and signifies the ability to achieve a determined set of business processes.

In this model, sets of business processes are described for employees in specific functional areas (such as sales). This is so as to establish appropriate work procedures and, consequently, a system that supports decision making at the strategic level, which includes an assessment of knowledge in an innovative company. This model is based on research results in companies (Fig. 3.7) (Patalas-Maliszewska and Werthner 2010).

In this model, the following conditions are formulated:

- A company consists of n-functionality areas: F_n, $n \in N$
- In each area, there are n-business processes: p_n, $n \in N$
- In each n-th area work, there are m-employees: m_n, $n,m \in N$
- Each m-th employee in a functional area can participate in more than one business process
- For each m-th employee in the functionality area, a personnel usefulness function can be defined: W_{nm}, $n,m \in N$

Based on my research results, a model for five employees in the sales area appears in Fig. 3.8.

The model in Fig. 3.8 shows the business processes in sales related to the personnel usefulness function. The presented model structure allows specification requirements in functional areas of the company, and it also permits an assessment of the success of employee selection. This model is the basis for building an assessment method for the value of strategic knowledge resources (knowledge workers), which in turns allows the selection of employees only for firms that are compatible with the given reference model.

3.2.3 Criteria Used to Describe an Innovative Company

An innovative company was described by Teece. A model showing the pace and direction of innovation at the company level appears in Fig. 3.9.

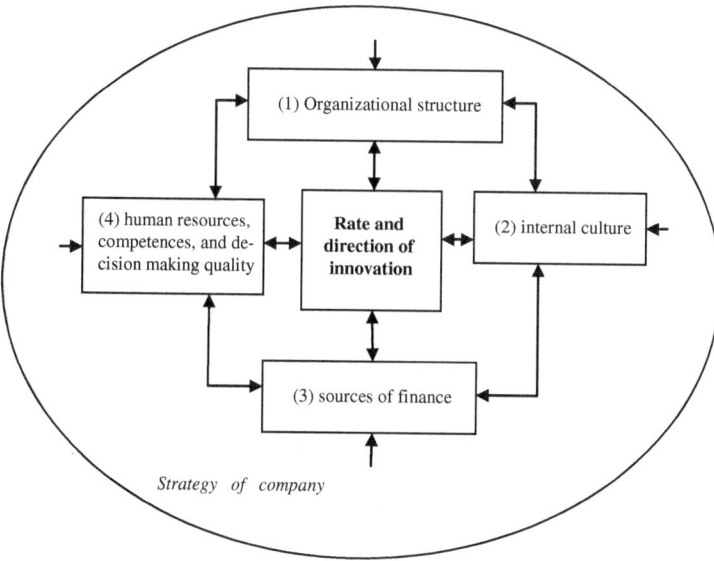

Fig. 3.9 Determinants of the rate and direction of innovation at the company level (Source: Teece 2002)

What actions will motivate the company to innovate?

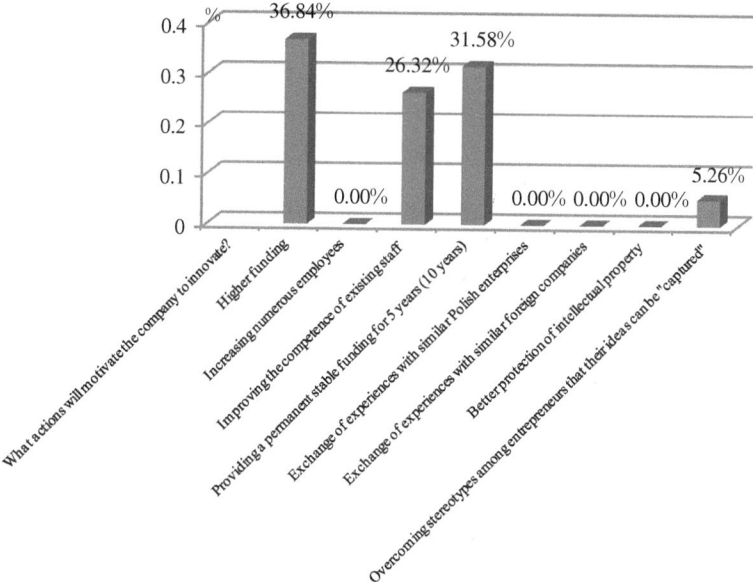

Fig. 3.10 Research results—activities that will encourage a company to introduce innovation

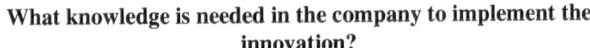

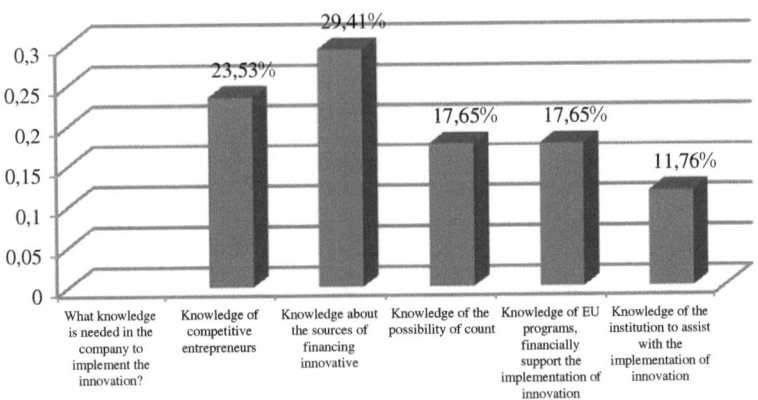

Fig. 3.11 Research results—what knowledge is needed implement innovation in a company?

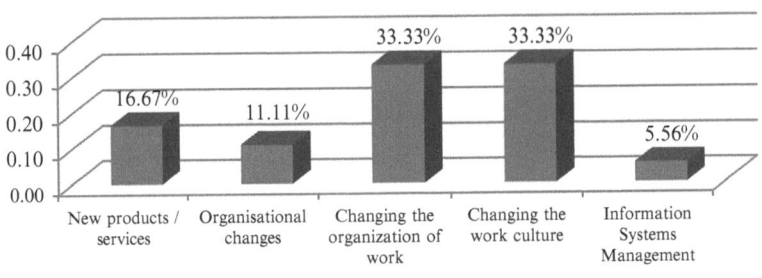

Fig. 3.12 Research results—the kinds of innovation needed in a company

Knowledge management is promoted as a necessary factor for organizational survival and maintenance of competitive strength. Organizations need good capacity to retain their employees and develop, organize, and utilize those employees' capabilities (Brennan and Connell 2000). Liu et al. suggested that taking advantage of knowledge management could stimulate employee potential and accelerate the integration of employee knowledge (Liu et al. 2001). Knowledge management has become a necessary condition for enterprises to survive in a competitive environment. Davenport and Prusak stated that knowledge management involves collecting and organizing information and transferring information to those that need it (Davenport and Prusak 1998). Drucker stated that "for each type of organization, transformation into an information-oriented organization is the best" (Drucker 1994).

It is now possible to define the values of selected determinants for establishing innovation within enterprises. Those indicators are defined based on model conditions concerning the pace and direction of innovation at the company level

(Fig. 3.8). The indicators are also defined based on preliminary studies carried out in 10 medium-sized Polish enterprises that operated in accordance with the accepted model of knowledge worker-oriented companies (see Sect. 3.2.2) The research was carried out by me on such a small group of companies because they were well matched for a complete study. I will use those results in defining the quantitative criteria that describe an innovative company. During the interviews that were conducted in that study, a number of questions were asked, including, "What will motivate this company to innovate?" (Fig. 3.10).

Among the respondents, 26 % felt that improving the competence of existing staff would allow the company to raise its level of innovation. The responses indicate the perceived importance of competence development as a method for improving the level of innovation in an enterprise.

In reply to the question "What knowledge is needed to implement innovation in the company?" 29 % of the respondents stated that the most important factor was knowledge about the sources of funding for innovation projects (Fig. 3.11).

These responses underline the significant impact of financial resources on innovation.

Another question was "What kind of innovation is needed in the company?" The responses to this question indicated that the interviewees recognized organizational culture and the structure of the company as being important in increasing the level of innovation (Fig. 3.12.).

I note that the empirical findings also point to main areas of business that affect the level of innovation in an enterprise (Fig. 3.9). Based on an analysis of the literature and on observations of economic reality, it is possible to define the quantitative criteria for an innovative company as follows:

- X_1—The share of new products and technologies in the value of annual sales:
  If $x_1 \in (0;0,5>$, it is set to 1, if $x_1 \in (0,5;1 >$ it is set to 2, if $x_1 \in (1;2 >$ it is set to 3, if $x_1 \in (2,3 >$ it is set to 4, if $x_1 \in (3,\infty >$ it is set to 5.
- X_2—The number of new products that have been implemented in a given year (for the last 5 years):
  If $x_2 \in (0;50>$, it is set to 1, if $x_1 \in (50;100 >$ it is set to 2, if $x_1 \in (100;200 >$ it is set to 3, if $x_1 \in (200,300 >$ it is set to 4, if $x_1 \in (300,\infty >$ it is set to 5.
- X_3—The number of new technologies implemented in a given year (for the last 5 years):
  If $x_3 \in (0;50>$, it is set to 1, if $x_3 \in (50;100 >$ it is set to 2, if $x_3 \in (100;200 >$ it is set to 3, if $x_3 \in (200,300 >$ it is set to 4, if $x_3 \in (300,\infty >$ it is set to 5.
- X_4—The number of completed research topics in a given year (for the last 5 years):
  If $x_4 \in (0;5>$, it is set to 1, if $x_4 \in (5;10 >$ it is set to 2, if $x_4 \in (10;20 >$ it is set to 3, if $x_4 \in (20,30 >$ it is set to 4, if $x_4 \in (30,\infty >$ it is set to 5.
- X_5—The number of patents in a given year (for the last 5 years):
  If $x_5 \in (0;5>$, it is set to 1, if $x_5 \in (5;10 >$ it is set to 2, if $x_5 \in (10;20 >$ it is set to 3, if $x_5 \in (20,30 >$ it is set to 4, if $x_5 \in (30,\infty >$ it is set to 5.

- X_6—The share of spending on research during the year to the value of sales:
  If $x_6 \in (0;0,05>$, it is set to 1, if $x_6 \in (0,05;0,2 >$ it is set to 2, if $x_6 \in (0,2;0,3 >$ it is set to 3, if $x_6 \in (0,3;0,4 >$ it is set to 4, if $x_6 \in (0,4;\infty >$ it is set to 5.
- X_7—The number of employees with science degrees:
  For a micro company:
  If $x_7 \in (0;1>$, it is set to 1, if $x_7 \in (1;2 >$ it is set to 2, if $x_7 \in (2;3 >$ it is set to 3, if $x_7 \in (3,4 >$ it is set to 4, if $x_7 \in (4,9 >$ it is set to 5.
  For a small company:
  If $x_7 \in (0;5>$, it is set to 1, if $x_7 \in (5;10 >$ it is set to 2, if $x_7 \in (10;20 >$ it is set to 3, if $x_7 \in (20,30 >$ it is set to 4, if $x_7 \in (30,49 >$ it is set to 5.
  For a medium-sized company:
  If $x_7 \in (0;10>$, it is set to 1, if $x_7 \in (10;20 >$ it is set to 2, if $x_7 \in (20;30 >$ it is set to 3, if $x_7 \in (30,50 >$ it is set to 4, if $x_7 \in (50,249 >$ it is set to 5.
- X_8—The number of employees with higher education in relation to other staff:
  If $x_8 \in (0;0,1>$, it is set to 1, if $x_8 \in (0,1;0,2 >$ it is set to 2, if $x_8 \in (0,2;0,3 >$ it is set to 3, if $x_8 \in (0,3;0,5 >$ it is set to 4, if $x_8 \in (0,5;1 >$ it is set to 5.
- X_9—The number of the company's scientific publications:
  If $x_9 \in (0;10>$, it is set to 1, if $x_9 \in (10;20 >$ it is set to 2, if $x_9 \in (20;30 >$ it is set to 3, if $x_9 \in (30;50 >$ it is set to 4, if $x_9 \in (50; \infty >$ it is set to 5.
- X_{10}—The number of awards received by the company in competitions:
  If $x_{10} \in (0;10>$, it is set to 1, if $x_{10} \in (10;20 >$ it is set to 2, if $x_{10} \in (20;30 >$ it is set to 3, if $x_{10} \in (30;50 >$ it is set to 4, if $x_{10} \in (50; \infty >$ it is set to 5.
- X_{11}—The number of sold licenses developed in a given year (for the last 5 years):
  If $x_{11} \in (0;1>$, it is set to 1, if $x_{11} \in (1;2 >$ it is set to 2, if $x_{11} \in (2;3 >$ it is set to 3, if $x_{11} \in (3;5 >$ it is set to 4, if $x_{11} \in (5; \infty >$ it is set to 5.
- X_{12}—The number of implementations of solutions developed in a given year (for the last 5 years):
  If $x_{12} \in (0;1>$, it is set to 1, if $x_{12} \in (1;2 >$ it is set to 2, if $x_{12} \in (2;3 >$ it is set to 3, if $x_{12} \in (3;5 >$ it is set to 4, if $x_{12} \in (5; \infty >$ it is set to 5.
- X_{13}—The number of purchased and used licenses:
  If $x_{13} \in (0;5>$, it is set to 1, if $x_{13} \in (5;10 >$ it is set to 2, if $x_{13} \in (10;20 >$ it is set to 3, if $x_{13} \in (20;30 >$ it is set to 4, if $x_{13} \in (30; \infty >$ it is set to 5.
  I can now define the model of an innovative company (Fig. 3.13).

The solution of a formulated problem (see Introduction) can be represented in the form of the following tasks. The first concerns the possibility of an objective selection (evaluation) of the knowledge worker; this assumes that the standard functional areas of the company in question and the associated business processes are well understood. The second refers to an assessment of the effectiveness of any investment in IC.

A procedure was developed to build a model for managing knowledge workers in a company. This procedure adopts the following key stages:

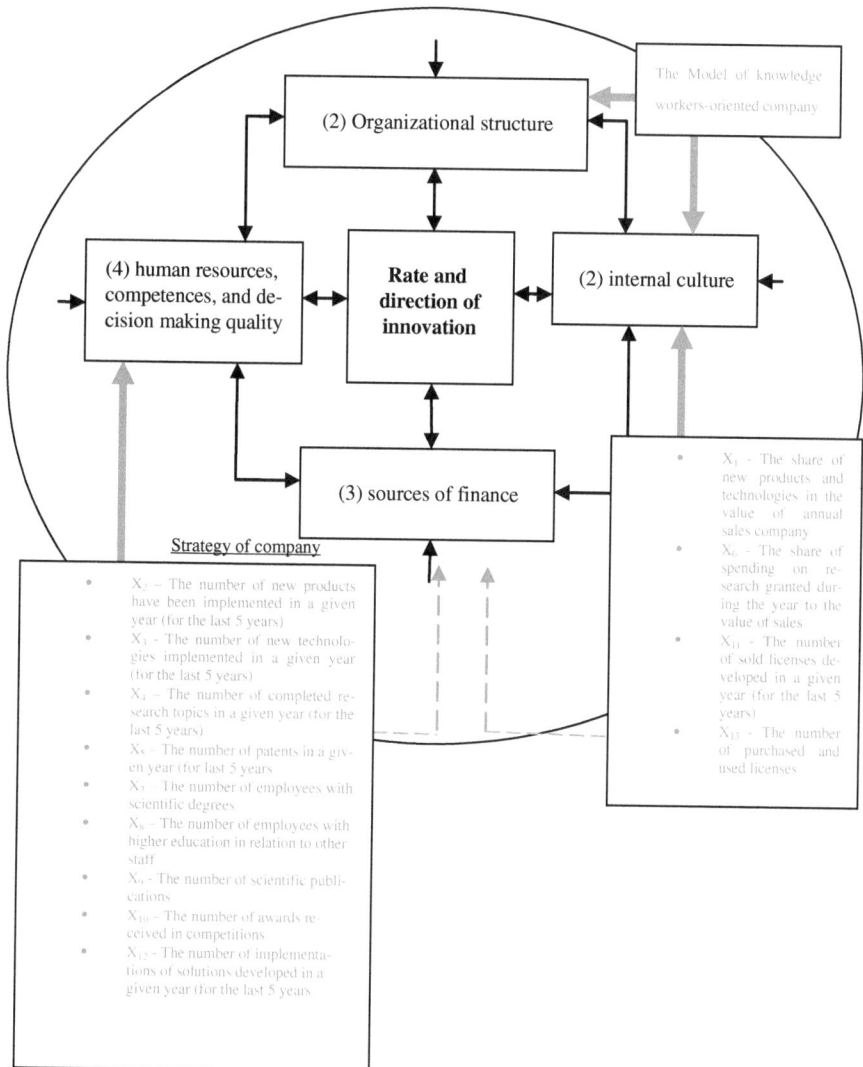

Fig. 3.13 A new concept of determinants of the rate and direction of company-level innovation

- Step 1: determine the structure of a hypothetical company
- Step 2: define the determinants of the innovative company
- Step 3: apply a multinomial model of decision making for the innovative company
- Step 4: determine the projected values of the usefulness personnel function for m-th employee in the company
- Step 5: determine the scheme of company in the employee-selection process

The next chapter presents the Sknowinnov method used for assessing the effectiveness of investments in IC in companies. It was built on the basis of a defined base value of indicators for the personnel usefulness function for the m-th employee in companies and the determinants of innovation using the Group Method of Data Handling. The base personnel usefulness function for the m-th employee, and the determinants of innovation were based on respondents' answers as a result of a number of surveys. One survey was conducted among 10 Polish companies that were consistent with the model of knowledge-worker oriented companies. The method used in that survey involved some determinants of innovation with the values of personnel usefulness function for the m-th employee in the company.

References

Aspen Institute Italia. (2007). *National interest: The showcases of excellence*. Aspen Institute Italia.

Baldridge, D. C., Floyd, S. W., & Markoczy, L. (2004). Are managers from Mars and academicians from Venus? Toward an understanding of the relationship between academic quality and practical relevance. *Strategic Management Journal, 25*(11), 1063–1074.

Barkema, H. G., & Vermeulen, F. (1998). International expansion through start-up or acquisition: A learning perspective. *Academy of Management Journal, 41*(1), 7–26.

Belbin, R. M. (2007). *Management teams: Why they succeed or fail*. Oxford: Elsevier Butterworth Heinemann.

Brennan, N., & Connell, B. (2000). Intellectual capital: Current issues and policy implications. *Journal of Intellectual Capital, 1*(3), 206–240.

Chakravarthy, B., Mueller-Stewens, G., Lorange, P., & Lechner, C. (Eds.). (2003). *Strategy process: Shaping the contours of the field*. Oxford: Blackwell.

Chandy, R. K., & Tellis, G. J. (2000). The incumbents curse—incumbency, size, and radical product innovation. *Journal of Marketing, 64*, 1–17.

Chen, Y. M., & Liang, M. W. (2000). Design and implementation of a collaborative engineering information system for allied concurrent engineering. *International Journal of Computer Integrated Manufacturing, 13*(1), 11–30

Child, J., & Faulkner, D. O. (1998). *Strategies of cooperation: managing alliances, networks, and joint ventures*. Oxford: Oxford University Press.

Davenport, T. H., & Prusak, L. (1998). *Working knowledge: How organizations manage what they know*. Boston: Harvard Business School Press.

Drucker, P. F. (1994). The age of social transformation. *The Atlantic Monthly*, 11, November 1994.

Dyer, J., & Singh, H. (1998). The relational view: Cooperative strategies and sources of interorganizational competitive advantage. *Academy of Management Review, 23*(4), 660–679.

Engelbrecht, H. J. (1997). International R&D spillovers, human capital and productivity in OECD economies: An empirical investigation. *European Economic Review, 41*, 1479–1488.

Farazmand, A. (2003). Chaos and transformation theories: A theoretical analysis with implications for organization theory and public management. *Public Organization Review: A Global Journal, 3*(4), 339–372.

Farazmand, A. (2004). *Building human capital for the 21st century: Strategic public personnel policy and management*. Westport: Praeger.

Furman, J. L., Porter, M. E., & Stern, S. (2002). The determinants of national innovative capacity. *Research Policy, 31*, 899–933.

Garvin, D. A. (2006). *Building the learning organization. Knowledge management*. Gliwice: Helion.

Green, S. G., Gavin, M. B., & Aiman-Smith, L. (1995). Assessing a multidimensional measure of radical technological innovation. *IEEE Transactions on Engineering Management, 42*(3), 203–214.

Grudzewski, W., & Hejduk, I. (2004). *Zarządzanie wiedzą w przedsiębiorstwach (Knowledge management in enterprises)*. Warszawa: PWN.

Gupta, J. H. D., Sharma, S. K., & Hsu, J. (2004). *An overview of knowledge management. Creating knowledge based organization*. London: Idea Grup.

Haas-Edersheim, E. (2007). *The definitive Drucker*. Warszawa: MT Biznes.

Hays, S. W., & Kearney, R. C. (2001). Anticipated changes in human resources management: Views from the field. *Public Administration Review, 61*(5), 585–592.

Hill, C. W. L., & Jones, G. R. (2000). *Strategic management: An integrated approach* (5th ed.). Boston: Houghton-Mifflin.

Hitt, M. A., Hoskisson, R. E., & Kim, H. (1997). International diversification: Effects on innovation and firm performance in product-diversified firms. *Academy of Management Journal, 40*(4), 767–798.

Hitt, M. A., Boyd, B. K., & Li, D. (2004). The state of strategic management research and a vision for the future. In B. Ketchen (Ed.), *Research methodology in strategic management* (pp. 1–31). Amsterdam: Elsevier.

INSEAD. (2007). *Global innovation index: More on methodology*. INSEAD Global Innovation Index

Institute for Management Development (2008). The IMD World Competitive Year Book, Lausanne, Switzerland.

Janz, N., & Peters, B. (2002). Innovation and innovation success in the German manufacturing sector, econometric evidence at firm level. Centre for European Economic Research (ZEW), Department of Industrial Economics and International Management, Mannheim.

Jasiński, H. (1992). *Innowacyjne przedsiębiorstwo (An innovative company of the market)*. Warszawa: KiW.

Kogut, B., & Zander, U. (1992). Knowledge of the firm, combinative capabilities, and the replication of technology. *Organization Science, 3*(3), 383–397.

Kotler, P. (1994). *Marketing management: Analysis, planning, implementation, and control*. Englewood Cliffs: Prentice Hall.

Koźmiński, A. K. (2002). How to build a knowledge-based economy? In G. W. Kolodko (Ed.), *Development of the Polish economy. Perspectives and conditions*. Warsaw: WSPiZ.

Liu, P. L., Yang, S. F., & Chen, W. C. (2001). The study of the implementation of knowledge management and its effects on increasing the competition. *Chung-Hua Journal of Management, 2*(1), 59–74.

Maier, R. (2002). *Knowledge management systems: Information and communication technologies for knowledge management*. Berlin: Springer.

Mikuła, B. (2002). *Zarządzanie przedsiębiorstwem w XXI wieku. Koncepcje i metody (Enterprises management in XXI. Concepts and methods)*. Warszawa: Difin.

Patalas, J., & Kłos, S. (2007). Knowledge management in SME in the Lubuskie province. In J. Lewandowsk, S. Kopera, & J. Królikowski (Eds.), *Information and knowledge in innovate enterprise* (pp. 81–87). Łódz/Poland.

Patalas-Maliszewska, J., & Werthner, H. (2010). Methodology of knowledge value assessment in an enterprise of SME sector. *Management and Production Engineering Review, 1*(1), 21–28.

Pedler, M., Burgoyne, J., & Boydell, T. (1996). *The learning company: A strategy for sustainable development*. London: McGraw-Hill.

Perechuda, K. (1997). *Wirtualne organizacje (Virtual organization)*. Wrocław: Ossolineum.

Perechuda, K. (2005). *Diffusion of knowledge in the enterprise network. Visualization and composition*. Economical University in Wrocław/Poland

Pisano, G. P., & Wheelwright, S. C. (1995). The new logic of high tech R&D. *Harvard Business Review, 73*(5), 93.

Pomykalski, A. (2001). *Zarządzanie innowacjami (Innovation management)*. Warszawa: PWN.

Porter, M. E. (1998). *Clusters and competition: New agendas for companies, governments, and institutions, on competition.* Boston: Harvard Business School Press.

Porter, M. E., & Stern, S. (1999). *The new challenge to America's prosperity: Findings from the innovation index.* Washington, DC: Council on Competitiveness.

Poznańska, K. (1998). *Innowacje w małych i średnich przedsiębiorstwach (Innovations in the small and medium sizes enterprises).* Dom Wydawniczy ABC / Warsaw/Poland

Rogers, E. M. (1995). *Diffusion of innovations.* New York: The free Press.

Romanowska, M., & Trocki, M. (Eds). (2004). *Process-oriented management.* Warsaw School of Economics. Warsaw, Poland.

Romjin, H., & Albaladejo, M. (2000). Determinants of innovation capability in small UK firms: An empirical analysis. Working paper, 40, University of Oxford, Queen Elizabeth House.

Sarkis, J., & Gunasekaran, A. (2003). Enterprise resource planning—Modelling and analysis. *European Journal of Operational Research, 146,* 229–232.

Schumpeter, J. A. (1939). *Business cycles: A theoretical, historical, and statistical analysis of the capitalist process.* New York/London: McGraw-Hill.

Senge, P. (1998). The practice of innovation. *Leader to leader, 1998*(9), 16–22.

Senge, P., Kleiner, A., Roberts, C., Ross, R., Roth, G., & Smith, B. (1999). *The dance of change: The challenges of sustaining momentum in learning organizations.* New York: Doubleday/ Currency.

Skyrne, D. J. (1999). *Knowledge networking.* Butterworth-Heinemann: Creating the collaborative enterprise.

Smith, B. L. R., & Barfield, C. E. (1996). *Technology, R&D, and the economy.* Washington, DC: The Brookings Institution.

Smith, A., & Rupp, W. (2002). Communication and loyalty among knowledge workers: A resource of the firm theory view. *Journal of Knowledge Management, 6*(3), 250–261.

Stabryła, A. (Ed.). (1991). *Doskonalenie struktur organizacyjnych (Improving the organizational structure).* Warszawa: PWE.

Stacey, R. D. (1992). *Managing the unknowable: Strategic boundaries between order and chaos in organizations.* San Francisco: Jossey-Bass.

Steinmann, H., & Schreyoegg, G. (2000). *Management (5th).* Wiesbaden: Gabler.

Stryjski, R., Krebs, I., & Kłos, S. (2008). *Innovation management in small and medium-sized enterprises: Development of innovation—experiences in Poland.* Berlin: Trafo.

Sveiby, K. E. (1997). *New organizational wealth: Managing and measuring knowledge-based assets.* San Francisco: Berrett Koehler.

Swan, J. A., Scarbrough, H., Preston, J. (1999). Knowledge management—The next fad to forget people? In Proceedings: 7th European conference on information systems, Vol. II (pp. 668–678). Copenhagen. 23–25 June 1999.

Teece, D. J. (2002). *Managing intellectual capital.* Oxford: Oxford University Press.

Teixeira, A. A. C., & Fortuna, N. (2006). Human capital, trade and long-run productivity. Testing the technological absorption hypothesis for the Portuguese economy, 1960–2001. FEP working papers, 226.

Utterback, J. M., & Abernathy, W. J. (1975). A dynamic model of process and product innovation. *The International Journal of Management Science, 3*(6), 639–656.

Vermuelen, F., & Barkema, H. (2001). Learning through acquisitions. *Academy of Management Journal, 44*(3), 457–476.

Walczak, S. (2005). Organizational knowledge management structure. *The Learning Organization, 12*(4), 330–339.

Watkins, K., & Marsick, V. (1992). Building the learning organization: A new role for human resource developers. *Studies in Continuing Education, 14*(2), 115–129.

Wei, C., & Wang, M. J. (2004). A comprehensive framework for selecting an ERP system. *International Journal of Project Management, 22,* 161–169.

Model for Managing Knowledge Workers

4

Assessing the status of knowledge in a company has to include methods of IC evaluation based on investment in the staff's knowledge development. However, there are no methods for assessing the efficiency of decisions with respect to acquiring knowledge. The literature distinguishes qualitative measures (e.g., the Danish Project of IC measurement; the Scandia Navigator; IAM; the IC-Rating model^{TM}; VCSTM; the Balanced Scorecard; Saratoga Institute Report) and methods of valuating IC (e.g., MV/MB indicator, Q-Tobin indicator, CIV indicator, KCE indicator, VAIC^{TM}, Economic Added Value, IAV model, Strassmann's method, IAMV^{TM}, Broker's Technology), as indicated in Chap. 2.

Ongoing attempts are being made to find methods for measuring IC, but there is still no widely accepted method for establishing an IC-assessment system. The difficulty is that the majority of the concepts have been formulated with respect to specific companies; the measuring methods have thus been tailor-made and do not permit general application. Because of the lack of concepts with respect to the assessment and forecasting value of knowledge workers in a company, the present study focuses on creating a method for assessing and predicting the value of knowledge workers in a company.

Many studies have focused on knowledge-management strategies from an organizational perspective (Barthelme et al. 1998; Basu 1998; Carayannis 1998; Drew 1999; Purser and Pasmore 1992; Studer et al. 1998). Sirmon and Hitt (2003) describe the primary processes for the effective management of resources in an organization. The first process is structuring the resource portfolio. This requires firms to engage in the acquisition and development of resources and, where necessary, removing less valuable resources. The second process entails bundling resources together to build unique, valuable capabilities.

Thus, describing knowledge workers as strategic-knowledge resources is motivated by the following:

- The concept of effective management of resources in an organization
- An enterprise's unique potential in the form of knowledge and experience (Barney 1995)
- The concept of competence management (Hamel and Prahalad 1994).

J. Patalas-Maliszewska, *Managing Knowledge Workers*, Management for Professionals,
DOI 10.1007/978-3-642-36600-0_4, © Springer-Verlag Berlin Heidelberg 2013

A strategic-knowledge resource in a company signifies the knowledge, skills, and capabilities of the individuals who make up the company's workforce. Such resources are usually reflected in a worker's education, experience, and specific identifiable skills (Hitt et al. 2001). Yet, how can resources be managed to create added value for an enterprise?

Makadok (2001) presented several stages in the management of a firm's resources. Sirmon and Hitt (2003) expanded Makadok's work to develop a model of how resources could be managed to create value. I will use the model of Sirmon and Hitt to examine five stages in the management of a firm's strategic-knowledge resources. These stages are identification, analysis, evaluation, configuring, and forecasting.

In this part of the monograph, I will present my method for assessing and forecasting the value of knowledge workers. Through a case study (assessing the value of the personnel usefulness function and the characteristics of innovation in ten companies), I will show how a matrix can be used to assess investment in knowledge. Subsequently, the concept of building a model supporting decision making will be presented; that model will allow the assessment and forecasting of knowledge workers in a company.

My research questions were as follows. Is it possible to describe the value of the knowledge of a given employee in an enterprise? Is there a method for assessing and predicting a knowledge worker's value in an enterprise?

4.1   Knowledge Workers as Strategic Knowledge Resources

4.1.1   Resource-Based Approach

As stated in the previous section, strategic-knowledge management is essential to achieving a competitive advantage (Hays and Kearney 2001). Purely operational measures—that is reactive rather than proactive, personal, and economic—are therefore inadequate as a means of differentiating one company from its competitors (Huselid et al. 1997). The theory of the resource-based view (RBV) appears to be appropriate as an economic theory for equally examining personnel policies and the impact of demographic changes (Boxall and Purcell 2000; Helfat and Peteraf 2003; Makadok 2001). The basic assumption of the RBV is that the individual organization's success is the result of the competition among heterogeneous resource endowments. In this respect, the focus is on those resources that have been developed within an organization. Only those resources can be a source of competitive advantage since they are tied to company-specific on a long-term basis (Argote and Ingram 2000; Barney and Zajac 1994; Lado and Wilson 1994). RBV researchers have already applied their methods to different business areas (Acedo et al. 2006).

The RBV is the result of the work of Penrose (1959); Wernerfelt (1984) presented his RBV of the firm, but the first comprehensive description of the RBV approach was published by Wright et al. (2001). Among others, Barney

(1991) focused on internal company resources (Prezewowsky 2007), and Barney established groundbreaking specifications that detailed how a competitive advantage could lead to resource properties (Wright et al. 2001). In the literature, there are very different definitions of the term "resource" for the purposes of the RBV. The various interpretations cover not only clarification of the terminology but also the categorization of resources and the attribution of resource properties and their contribution to competitive positions. Lado and Wilson summarized the findings in the literature: they stated that a company is a network of resources and skills and that potential sources of sustainable competitive advantage exist if the economic benefits provided by the company's services are not fully replicated by competitors' activities (Lado and Wilson 1994).

The term "resource-based" refers to the total competitive success of a company's underlying resources and combinations of its resources. These resources must however meet certain characteristics—in recent years in the literature as follows:

- Nolte and Bergmann (1998): durability, usability, relative rarity, rarity, transferability, substitutability, inimitability, ambiguity, specificity, complexity, tacitness, historicity
- Barney (2001): value, rareness, imperfect imitability, substitutability
- Grant (1997): durability, transparency, transferability, replicability
- Eriksen and Mikkelsen (1996): value, heterogeneity, imitability, substitutability
- Smart and Wolfe, (2000): value, strategic relevance, sustainability, mobility, inimitability, substitutability, strategic flexibility

The differences among the authors may be the result of different levels of detail in their definition.

The RBV assumes that this heterogeneity and the result of entrepreneurial activity are due to the uneven distribution of resources. At the same time, this resource heterogeneity does not take into account microeconomic considerations owing to the fact that these company-specific resources rely on imbalances in the market and involve high transaction costs (Barney 1991). The competitive advantages relate more to a company's use of equipment and resources than to its product-market position (Lado and Wilson 1994).

The positive results of the RBV have been emphasized in relevant studies (Colbert 2004; Wright et al. 2001; Freiling 2001; Führing 2006).

These positive features include wide, rapid dissemination in the scientific literature and in management practices; they also include the heterogeneous character of the RBV, such that different theories and perspectives can be integrated within it, which adds to its status as primarily a strategic management approach (Acedo et al. 2006). The great advantage of the RBV over the prevailing market-based view is that it assesses competitive success primarily in terms of specific market situations and the corporate potential for creating mutually dependent relationships (Prezewowsky 2007). With the increasing complexity and dynamic character of the business environment, the possibilities of developmental analysis, and lack of predictability with regard to influencing environmental factors, it is important to examine strategically relevant internal factors in a business that would allow a prediction of success. However, discussions about the methodical status of the RBV are incomplete. The criticism has been leveled that too few efforts have been made for a theoretical structure for the RBV to be developed (Priem and Butler 2001). In particular, the long-existing confusion about dealing with resources and understanding the terminology assumptions have led to further censure of the RBV. Many studies have been based on the RBV; however, the use of the frequency range has been presented as an argument for its empirical validity (Barney 2001).

The lack of analytical and empirical foundations for classifying and defining human resources as strategic assets in recent years was discussed by Prezewowsky (2007). Uncertainty has led to difficulties in the practical use of resources. However, it has been noted that the very lack of appropriate tools "to implement a resource-oriented management" is a cause for concern (Boos and Jarmai 1994).

Criticism about the static nature of conventional RBV has been reflected in the fact that through constant changes in the environment, companies are forced to adjust their resource endowments, reconfigure, and stabilize (Becker 2004; Pfeffer and Salancik 1978; Priem and Butler 2001). This resulted in the dynamic capabilities approach. "Dynamic" here relates to the ability to adapt to a changing business environment; "capabilities" emphasizes the key role of strategic management and the internal and external perception of organizational skills (Teece et al. 1997). In turn is carried out by individuals primarily through organizational learning processes.

It is often stated in the literature that there is a need for an efficient, robust tool that is capable of measuring the value of employees. A proper solution to this urgent question is long overdue.

Resources are important to a firm's performance; however, according to the RBV, whether an organization gains a competitive advantage and any associated returns depends on the strategic planning used to leverage those resources (Chrisman et al. 2003; McGrath and MacMillan 2000).

The need to describe knowledge workers as a strategic-knowledge resource is motivated by the concept of resource management and competence management (Fig. 4.1) (Patalas-Maliszewska and Hochmeister 2011).

Here, I will briefly describe competence management in a company. The significance of competence management in knowledge-intensive businesses is well established. As a subdivision of knowledge management, competence management deals with the knowledge of individuals, i.e., their competences. The capabilities of individuals in accomplishing a task are often referred to using such terms as qualifications, skills, and competences. However, an explicit difference is made in the literature between these concepts. The concept of competence is represented by a combination of knowledge, behavior, and skills that give an individual the potential to perform a task effectively (Draganidis and Mentzas 2006; Penner-Hahn and Shaver 2005).

The aim of competence management is to plan, implement, and evaluate initiatives that ensure that the proper competences are available to a company, thereby allowing it to achieve its business objectives (Nordhaug 1993). To support this task, Berio and Harzallah (2005) define four processes for competence management:

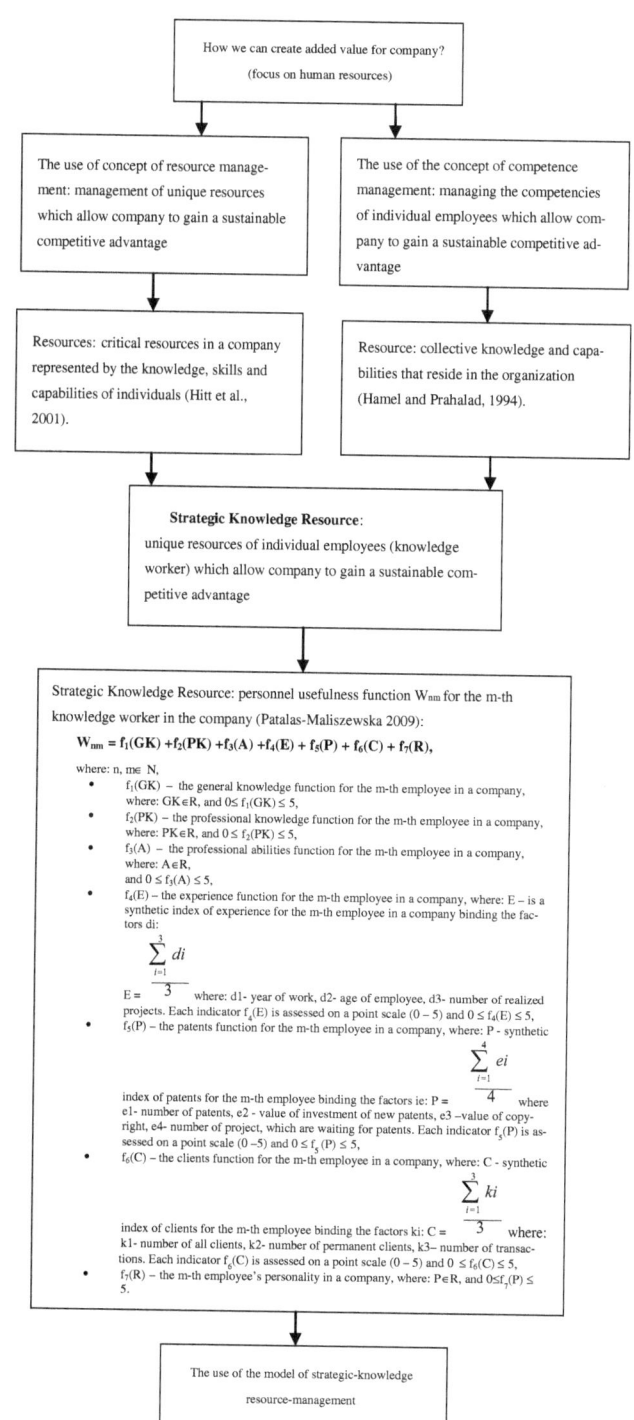

Fig. 4.1 Definition of strategic-knowledge resources in a company (Source: Patalas-Maliszewska and Hochmeister 2011)

- Competence identification—defining the required competence
- Competence assessment—determining whether a competence has been acquired
- Competence acquisition—planning how required competences can be acquired
- Competence usage—systematically utilizing knowledge about competences for the benefit of an organization

For a company to preserve its competitive edge, it is necessary to develop a competence-management system. In general terms, competence management operates on two levels—the macro and the micro. The former is concerned with core competences and is controlled by business management. Thus, a core competence is understood as signifying the total collective knowledge and capabilities that reside in an organization (Hamel and Prahalad 1994). On the micro level, led by human-resource management, the focus lies on the competences of individual employees. The competences a company requires to meet its strategic goals are transformed from the macro to the micro level. Conversely, existing competences on the micro level are exchanged via business management to support strategy design.

I distinguish the value of knowledge workers—specialists in selling—as follows: m1, sales director; m2, sales specialist; m3, marketing specialist; m4, regional assistant; and m5, product manager—the list has been already presented in Sect. 3.2.2. I do this using the personnel usefulness function (Patalas-Maliszewska 2011).

4.1.2   Personnel Usefulness Function for a Knowledge Worker

I define here the personnel usefulness function, W_{nm}, for the m-th knowledge worker in the n-th functional area in a company:

$$W_{nm} = f(GK, \ PK, \ A, \ E, \ P, \ C, \ R),$$

where n, m$\in$N and:
- GK—general knowledge of the m-th employee. The value of this parameter is obtained through the results of tests for employees; it is evaluated in the range of 1–5, where 1 is a poor and 5 a very good level of general knowledge.
- PK—professional knowledge of the m-th employee. The value of this parameter is obtained through the results of tests for employees; it is evaluated in the range of 1–5, where 1 is a poor and 5 a very good level of professional knowledge.
- A—professional abilities of the m-th employee. The value of this parameter is obtained through the results of tests for employees; it is evaluated in the range of 1–5, where 1 is a poor and 5 a very good level of professional abilities.
- E—experience of the m-th employee. The value of this parameter is obtained through tests for employees; it is evaluated within the range of 1–5, where 1 is a poor and 5 a very good level of experience.

- P—patents of the m-th employee. The value of this parameter is obtained through the results of tests for employees; it is evaluated within the range of 1–5, where 1 is a poor and 5 a very good level of patents.
- C—clients of the m-th employee. The value of this parameter is obtained through the results of tests for employees; it is evaluated within the range of 1–5, where 1 is a poor and 5 a very good level of clients.
- R—personality of the m-th employee. The value of this parameter is obtained through the results of tests for employees; it is evaluated within the range of 1–5, where 1 is a poor and 5 a very good level of personality.

Effectiveness is measured in terms of degree. It is achieved in systems in which planning and efficiency are also defined by degree (Kosieradzka and Lis 2000). Thus, parameters E, P, and C are related to effectiveness; parameters GK, PK, A, and R are related to efficiency.

The following personnel usefulness function, W_{nm}, for the m-th knowledge worker in the company is proposed:

$$W_{nm} = f_1(GK) + f_2(PK) + f_3(A) + f_4(E) + f_5(P) + f_6(C) + f_7(R),$$

where n, m $\in$ N.

The linear form of this function, W_{nm}, is chosen because all elements are independent and equally important in assessing the effectiveness and efficiency of investment in knowledge:

- $f_1(GK)$—the general knowledge function for the m-th employee in a company, where $GK \in R$, and $1 \leq f_1(GK) \leq 5$.
- $f_2(PK)$—the professional knowledge function for the m-th employee in a company, where $PK \in R$, and $1 \leq f_2(PK) \leq 5$.
- $f_3(A)$—the professional abilities function for the m-th employee in a company, where $A \in R$, and $1 \leq f_3(A) \leq 5$.
- $f_4(E)$—the experience function for the m-th employee in a company, where E is a synthetic index of experience for the m-th employee in a company binding the

  factors ei: $E = \dfrac{\sum_{i=1}^{3} di}{3}$, where e1—year of work; e2—age of employee; e3—number of realized projects. Each indicator $f_4(E)$ is assessed on a points scale (1–5) and $1 \leq f_4(E) \leq 5$.
- $f_5(P)$—the patents function for the m-th employee in a company, where P—

  synthetic index of patents for the m-th employee binding the factors pi: $P = \dfrac{\sum_{i=1}^{4} ei}{4}$ where p1—number of patents; p2—value of investment of new patents; p3—value of copyrights; p4—number of projects that are awaiting patents. Each indicator $f_5(P)$ is assessed on a points scale (1–5) and $1 \leq f_5(P) \leq 5$.
- $f_6(C)$—the clients function for the m-th employee in a company, where C—

  synthetic index of clients for the m-th employee binding the factors ci: $C = \dfrac{\sum_{i=1}^{3} ki}{3}$

where c1—number of all clients; c2—number of permanent clients; c3—number of transactions. Each indicator $f_6(C)$ is assessed on a points scale (1–5) and $1 \leq f_6(C) \leq 5$.

- $f_7(R)$—the m-th employee's personality in a company, where $P \in R$ and $1 \leq f_7(P) \leq 5$.

It is possible to obtain the necessary data for evaluating the personnel usefulness function from knowledge worker-oriented companies through interviews conducted at each enterprise. Each knowledge worker completes the questionnaire. Using an algorithm to test solutions for each employee, it is possible to determine a specific value for the personnel usefulness function and each of the parameters pertaining to this function. I present here an algorithm for obtaining the value function.

I would like to note that the substantive content of the following tests can be modified to meet the requirements of a given workplace in a management company. The following example shows only one set of possible questions to demonstrate the applicability of this function, W_{nm}.

4.1.2.1 f_1(GK): General Knowledge Function for the m-th Knowledge Worker in a Company

To obtain the value for f_1(GK), the m-th employee completes the following test. This is an example of my verification test for general knowledge of the m-th employee in the sales area.

Test (GK):
1. For marketing resources should not be:
   - Price
   - Demand
   - Product
   - Promotion
2. The life cycle of a product/service is:
   - The appearance of the product
   - Product quality
   - The length of the product life
   - Change in product prices
3. Product mix:
   - The set of all product lines
   - A collection of only one type of product
   - A collection of products aimed at a market
   - A collection of products with the same price
4. Distribution channels are different:
   - Market channels
   - Strategic channels
   - Economic channels
   - Production channels

5. Advertising is:
   - Any form of nonpersonal presentation and promotion of the product (service)
   - Paying for an impersonal form of presentation and promotion of the product (service)
   - Short-term action to boost sales of the product (service)
   - Any action aimed at promoting the product (service)
6. Direct marketing is:
   - Personal and direct presentation of the product (service)
   - Any form of nonpersonal presentation and promotion of the product (service)
   - Customer relationship management
   - The use of nonpersonal contact tools to communicate with the client
7. Sales promotion is:
   - Short-term action to boost sales of the product (service)
   - The planned long-term promotion of a product (service)
   - Measures to promote the product (service) conducted via the Internet
   - Measures to promote the product (service) conducted by telephone
8. Public relations is:
   - Promotion of products (services) in the media without permission
   - Planned promotion campaign in the media
   - The long-term promotion of products (services) in the media
   - Any action aimed at promoting the product (service)
9. Carrying out activities aimed at building a strategy for the company is important because:
   - Does not allow long-term development of the company in an industry
   - Anticipated change in the business environment
   - Does not allow development in conditions of increasing competition
   - Allows the elimination of the risk of misdiagnosis of business development
10. Asset-enterprise strength is not:
    - The possibility of extending the range
    - Good reputation with customers
    - Being recognized as a market leader
    - Experienced management team

To obtain the value of $f_1(GK)$ we employ an algorithm:
- If a user has 5 or fewer correct answers: 1 point
- If a user has 6 correct answers: 2 points
- If a user has 7 correct answers: 3 points
- If a user has 8 correct answers: 4 points
- If a user has 9–10 correct answers: 5 points

4.1.2.2 $f_2(PK)$: The Professional Knowledge Function for the m-th Knowledge Worker in a Company

To obtain the value for $f_2(PK)$, the m-th employee completes the following test (an example of the author's verification test of professional knowledge for the m-th employee in the sales area):

Test (PK):
1. Does the company intend to launch a new product on the market?
    – Yes
    – No
    – I do not know
2. Does the company intend to change the user market?
    – Yes
    – No
    – I do not know
3. Does the company want to introduce new sales channels?
    – Yes
    – No
    – I do not know
4. Does the company want to enter new markets?
    – Yes
    – No
    – I do not know
5. Does the customer have an exclusive supply provider?
    – Yes
    – No
    – I do not know
6. Is the client sensitive to price changes?
    – Yes
    – No
    – I do not know
7. Does the client use the supplier's Web site?
    – Yes
    – No
    – I do not know
8. Is the customer satisfied with the work of the supplier's sales offices?
    – Yes
    – No
    – I do not know
9. Is the customer satisfied with the terms of vendor contracts?
    – Yes
    – No
    – I do not know
10. Is the customer kept informed about changes in the company?
    – Yes
    – No
    – I do not know
    The value of $f_2(\textbf{PK})$ is obtained from an algorithm:
- If there are 7–10 "I do not know" answers: 1 point
- If there are 5–6 "I do not know" answers: 2 points
- If there are 4 "I do not know" answers: 3 points

- If there are 2–3 "I do not know" answers: 4 points
- If there are 0–1 "I do not know" answers: 5 points

4.1.2.3 f₃(A): Professional Abilities Function for the m-th Knowledge Worker in a Company

To obtain the value for $f_3(A)$, the m-th employee completes the following table (an example of the author's verification test of abilities for employee in the sales area):

Table (A)

	Occasionally	Sometimes	Often	Very often	Always
I represent the interests of the client's in my own company					
I maintain contacts with customers after the sale					
I supplement knowledge about changes of product range in my company's					
I inform customers about changes in the market					
I supplement knowledge about changes in product mix at the customer					
I prepare to talk to my customers					
I lead discussions with clients					

The value of $f_3(A)$ is obtained from an algorithm:
- If there are 5–7 "occasionally" answers: 1 point
- If there are 4 "occasionally" answers: 2 points
- If there are 3 "occasionally" answers: 3 points
- If there are 2 "occasionally" answers: 4 points
- If there is 1 "occasionally" answer: 5 points

4.1.2.4 f₄(E): Experience Function for the m-th Knowledge Worker in a Company

To obtain the value for $f_4(E)$, the m-th employee completes the following table (an example of the author's verification test of experience of the m-th employee in the sales area):

Table $f_4(E)$:

e_1—number of years in a company
e_2—an age
e_3—the number of my ideas realized

The value of $f_4(E)$ is obtained from an algorithm E:

$$\frac{\sum_{i=1}^{3} ei}{3}$$

where e_1—number of years in business, e_2—age, e_3—the number of my ideas realized.

- If there are 25 or fewer points: 1 point
- If there are 26–40 points: 2 points
- If there are 41–50 points: 3 points
- If there are 51–60 points 4 point
- If there are over 60 points: 5 points

4.1.2.5 $f_5(P)$: Patents Function for the m-th Knowledge Worker in a Company

To obtain the value for $f_5(P)$, the m-th employee completes the following table (an example of the author's verification test of patents experience for the m-th employee in the sales area):

Table $f_5(P)$:

p_1—the value of my patents
p_2—the number of my patents
p_3—the value of my copyright
p_4—the number of my projects pending patent

The value of $f_5(P)$ is obtained from an algorithm P:

$$\frac{\sum_{i=1}^{4} ei}{4}$$

where p_1—the value of my patents, p_2—the number of my patents, p_3—the value of my copyright, p_4—the number of my projects pending patent.

- If there are 0 points: 1 point
- If there are over 0 points: 5 points

4.1.2.6 $f_6(C)$: Clients Function for the m-th Knowledge Worker in a Company

To obtain the value for $f_6(C)$, the m-th employee completes the following table (an example of the author's verification test of the m-th employee's relationship with clients in the sales area):

Table $f_6(C)$:

c_1—the number of my customers
c_2—the number of my regular customers
c_3—the number of my transactions (such as auction business documents, contracts, acquired clients)/month

The value of $f_6(C)$ is obtained from an algorithm:

- If any answer is given: 1 point
- If only the answer "the number of my customers" is given: 2 points

- If only the answer "the number of my regular customers" is given: 3 points
- If 2 answers are given: 4 points
- If 3 answers are given: 5 points

4.1.2.7 $f_7(R)$ m-th Knowledge Worker's Personality in a Company

To obtain the value for $f_7(R)$, the m-th employee completes the following table (an example of the test of the m-th employee's personality in the sales area):

Table (R) based on the Nosal 2002:

I care more about	The feelings of people	Their rights
I am usually more comfortable with people	Who are gifted with imagination	Who are realists
A bigger compliment is to define someone as	Influencing other people	A rationally thinking person
If I do something together with many people, it is more important for me	To act in an acceptable manner	To find my own course of action
I am more irritated by	Theorists	Extreme practitioners
Higher praise should be given to someone	With vision	With common sense
With me, it is more for	My heart to rule my head	My head to rule my heart
I think a bigger mistake is	An excessive display of warm feelings	Not being simpatico
If I were a teacher, I would prefer to teach:	Theoretical subjects	Subjects based on important facts
Which word appeals to you more?	Compassion	Predictability
Which word appeals to you more?	Justice	Pity
Which word appeals to you more?	Production	Project
Which word appeals to you more?	Mild	Firm
Which word appeals to you more?	Indiscriminate	Critical
Which word appeals to you more?	Literal	Figurative
Which word appeals to you more?	Ingenious	Practical

The value of $f_7(R)$ is obtained from an algorithm:
- Sensitive: 2b, 4a, 5a, 6b, 9b, 12a, 15a, 16b
- Intuition: 2a, 4b, 5b, 6a, 9a, 12b, 15b, 16a
- Thinking: 1b, 3b, 7b, 8a, 10b, 11a, 13b, 14b
- Feelings: 1a, 3a, 7a, 8b, 10a, 11b, 13a, 14a
  Interpretation of results:
- Indication of intuition: if the intuition total is equal to or more than the senses total
- Indication of senses: if senses total is greater than the intuition total
- Indication of feelings: if the feelings total is equal to or greater than the thinking total
- Indication of thinking: if the thinking total is greater than the feelings total
  (The two highest of the above scores are chosen and in accordance with the model of a knowledge worker-oriented company):

- If you are a sales director/product manager and senses are indicated: 5 points.
- If you are a sales director/product manager and intuition is indicated: 1 point.
- If you are a sales director/product manager and thinking is indicated: 3 points.
- If you are a sales director/product manager and feelings are indicated: 2 points.
- If you are a sales specialist/regional assistant and senses are indicated: 3 points.
- If you are a sales specialist/regional assistant and intuition is indicated: 5 points.
- If you are a sales specialist/regional assistant and thinking is indicated: 1 point.
- If you are a sales specialist/regional assistant and feelings are indicated: 2 points.
- If you are a marketing specialist and the senses are indicated: 1 point.
- If you are a marketing specialist and intuition is indicated: 1 point.
- If you are marketing specialist and thinking is indicated: 2 points.
- If you are a marketing specialist and feelings are indicated: 5 points.
- If you are a regional assistant and the senses are indicated: 4 points.
- If you are a regional assistant and intuition is indicated: 1 point.
- If you are a regional assistant and thinking is indicated: 3 points.
- If you are a regional assistant and feelings are indicated: 1 point.
- If you are a product manager and the senses are indicated: 4 points.
- If you are a product manager and intuition are indicated: 1 point.
- If you are a product manager and thinking is indicated: 2 points.
- If you are a product manager and feelings are indicated: 5 points.

After the various parameters are obtained for the knowledge worker, the value of the personnel usefulness function is obtained as follows:

$$W_{nm} = f_1(GK) + f_2(PK) + f_3(A) + f_4(E) + f_5(P) + f_6(C) + f_7(R)$$

where n, m $\in$ N.

It should be noted that the proposed approach for measuring the personnel usefulness function offers an estimated value of the knowledge workers in a company. The personnel usefulness function may be used as complement to traditional means of valuation in a company, which are usually based on the value of tangible assets. Still, the problem remains unsolved: it is not possible to assign individual workers to future revenue streams in an organization because such streams arise as a result of human interaction with the work.

One of the instruments used in knowledge management is knowledge of an individual. The proposed personnel usefulness function may be treated as an extension of knowledge management in an organization (according to the concept of Maier 2002). It is necessary to map the sources of knowledge, management expertise, and experience of the individual.

The value function may be useful to determine the amount of IC in organizations based on the personal usefulness function and the individual value of each knowledge worker. The proposed approach with the personal usefulness function amounts to adjusting the measurements to a specific job and company characteristics.

The personnel usefulness function introduced in this section offers more possibilities in the area of knowledge profitability. Beyond being a basic calculation of investment profitability, this approach appears to be an excellent tool for analyzing a knowledge worker's value. I will now describe conventional methods of employment planning and selection to demonstrate that there is a gap in the methods of planning and evaluation of knowledge workers in terms of their innovation level in a company.

4.2 Methods of Employment Planning and Selection

Management of potential social organizations requires definitions of the elements and tools for implementing personnel function. Personnel function in a company covers all matters relating to the people in the organization, including their acquisition, management, and professional development. It has been proposed that regulatory activities under this function (planning, organizing, motivating, and controlling) be referred to as personnel management (Lichtarski 2000; Studer et al. 1998; Perry et al. 1996; Krämer et al. 2005).

The role of the personnel function has evolved from an operational to a strategic one. This role has been as follows: (1) operational—administration of payroll in the company (1900–1945); (2) managerial (tactical)—bearing responsibility for administration and recruitment, maintenance of relationships with the labor market (1945–1980); (3) strategy-including the formulation of human resources strategy (since 1980) (Król and Ludwiczyński 2007). The personnel function is undergoing continual development for the following reasons: increased international competition; the size and complexity of modern enterprises; higher level of workforce education; changing workforce demographics (greater participation of women and ethnic minorities in the workforce).

Employment plans in enterprises should reflect the demand for labor in terms of qualitative and quantitative criteria for evaluating employees and the manner and form of motivating those employees. The selection of appropriate employment planning methods depends on several key factors: the planning horizon, sources of information used in the planning process, the cost of applying the method.

In the literature, different methods of planning divisions of employment are given: (1) analytical and descriptive methods, and (2) statistical methods. The first group includes the following:

- Managerial assessment—a method of forecasting the demand for human resources (Armstrong 2001). It is assumed that managers understand personnel needs best. Data collected from managers are subject to gradual aggregation. This method can be carried using a top-down approach: employment forecasts are prepared by top management and then agreed upon and presented to lower-level managers. It can also be carried using a bottom-up approach: the lowest-level managers prepare information on staff demand in their area, and this is forwarded to top management.
- Delphi method—this involves setting up a group of experts, who draw up views on the supply and demand of human resources (King 2007).

- Benchmarking method—this determines the demand for workers on the basis of information about employment in the best companies of a similar profile (Ramos-Rodriguez and Ruiz-Navarro 2004).
- Forecasting the zero-based –this takes as a starting point the current state of employment, but every year the base is adjusted and updated. If there is a need for hiring an employee, checks are made against this base as to whether the move is justified (Kostera 2000).
- Indicator method—there are set percentages (numbers) for individual professional groups within the company as a part of total employment (McKenna and Beech 1997).
- Method proposed by labor standards—time, performance, handling, and stocking. Depending on the solutions contained in the system and the standardization of work, the necessary employment in the company can be calculated (Pawlak 2003).

The second group includes the following:

- Statistical analysis—using past data and inputting them into the forecast. Prognostic variables are those factors that have had an impact on employment in the past, such as sales volume and productivity (Gajek and Kałuszka 2000)
- Markov analysis—historical trends are treated as the base from which to formulate future proposals (Szałkowski 2002)
- Scenario forecasting—creative planning that involves preparing several scenarios of events (Sekuła 2001)
- Computer simulation—experimenting with possible and probable situations (Szałkowski 2002)

The skilful use of different instruments in shaping employment in an organization requires management and the human resource professionals to operate in their respective spheres of competence. The employee-selection process comprises all activities that are aimed at hiring competent employees, whose work should contribute to the mission and goals of the organization (Pawlak 2003). The following methods are notable in the employee-selection process: (1) internal recruitment—advertisements in the intranet, reserve personnel, list of success stories, contests; (2) external recruitment—advertisements in the press, Internet, radio, television, employee recommendations, employment agencies, universities; (3) selection—analysis of documents, interviews, tests, assessment center, unconventional methods, such as astrology; (4) adaptation—preliminary evaluation of the employee.

I have attempted to develop a method for forecasting and selecting knowledge workers in a company: the Sknowinnov method. This method contains elements of benchmarking methods, statistical analysis, and Markov analysis and the tests used in employee-selection methods. The Sknowinnov method allows the evaluation of candidates according to accepted examination criteria and is in line with the strategic objectives of a company in terms of innovation.

4.3 New Concept for Planning and Assessing Knowledge Workers

4.3.1 Sknowinnov Method for Assessing the Value of Knowledge Workers

The decision about selecting appropriate knowledge workers requires that the company management assess the efficiency of the investment. The application of the Sknowinnov method makes it possible to obtain a forecast of the value of a knowledge worker.

This research was motivated by the actual need of manager, who had a strong desire to improve his own company's innovation level through selecting knowledge workers. This research thus began with a literature review of employee-selection methods and definitions of knowledge workers. Next, based upon empirical research in Polish companies, the Sknowinnov method and polynomial models of decision making ("the best polynomials") for individual knowledge workers (m1, m2, m3, m4, and m5) was created. The method allows a multi-criteria evaluation of the effectiveness of knowledge-worker selection in a company.

The Sknowinnov method consists of four elements (Patalas-Maliszewska 2009; Patalas-Maliszewska and Werthner 2010):

- Experience in companies regarding investment in knowledge: research results (sets of business processes are created for the m-th knowledge worker in the n-th functionality area, for example the sales area in a company; see Sect. 3.2.2)
- Indicator matrix to assess the effectiveness and efficiency of investment in knowledge workers: research results from ten companies (value of the personnel usefulness function).
- Innovation: values of the characteristics of innovation in a company—see Chap. 3: research results from ten companies
- The group data handling method (GMDH) algorithm (Farlow 1984)
  Figure 4.2 presents an overview of the Sknowinnov method.

4.3.1.1 Indicator Matrix to Assess the Effectiveness and Efficiency of Investment in Knowledge Workers: Research Results from Ten Companies

The indicator matrix is proposed based on the literature and my own research. The matrix will help in assessing the effectiveness of knowledge worker selection in a company. The indicators (values of personnel usefulness function) include measures to show the value of knowledge workers in a company.

The next step involves a survey of selected companies (research focus group), which was done by conducting interviews in ten companies that conformed to the model of a knowledge worker-oriented company. Based on the results of research in the sales area in companies (the research group consisted of ten companies that conformed to the concrete model of an enterprise; see Sect. 3.2.2), the values of the

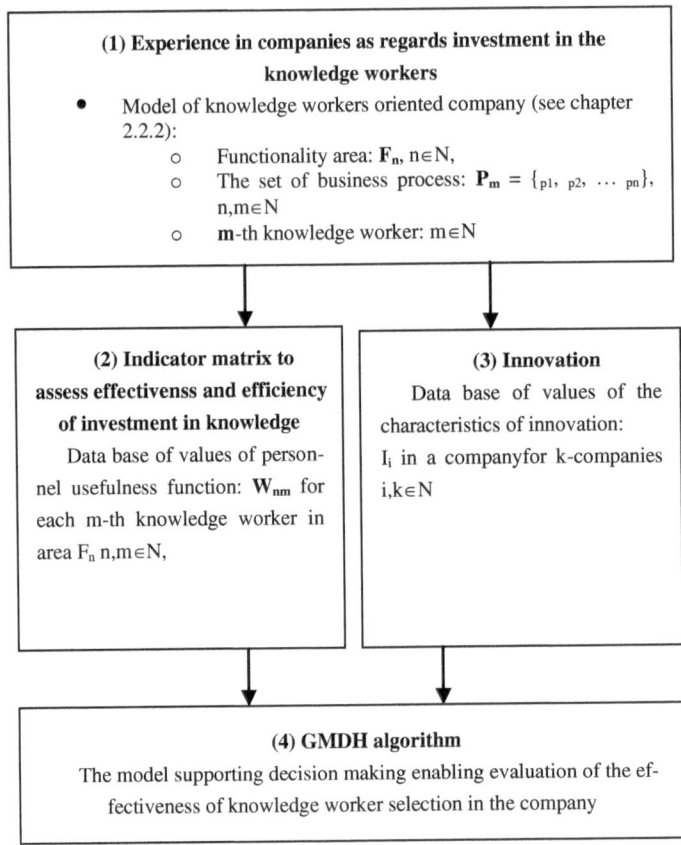

Fig. 4.2 Sknowinnov method

personnel usefulness function for five knowledge workers (m = 5) were assessed: m_1, sales director; m_2, sales specialist; m_3, marketing specialist; m_4, regional assistant; m_5, product manager. This was carried out in the sales area (n = 1) in each of the ten companies (matrix of the personnel usefulness function)—Tables 4.1 and 4.2.

To determine whether the result is good for a given enterprise, it is necessary to compare that result with the values for the sales department for each employee of another enterprise according to the reference model. Next, we can consider if the present condition of IC is satisfactory.

Figure 4.3 presents example of the values of the personnel usefulness function in the sales area in ten companies for a sales specialist based on the research results.

We can compare the value of the personnel usefulness function in the sales area for a sales specialist and the best result received for an employee in ten companies.

Table 4.1 Values of the personnel usefulness function in the sales area in ten companies: the matrix of the personnel usefulness function for five knowledge workers (m = 5) in the sales area (n = 1) in ten companies

Company/sale area	m_1 Sales director	m_2 Sales specialist	m_3 Marketing specialist	m_4 Regional assistant	m_5 Product manager
C1/1	$W_{C1/11} = 25$	$W_{C1/12} = 4$	$W_{C1/13} = 12$	$W_{C1/14} = 13$	$W_{C1/15} = 16$
C2/1	$W_{C2/11} = 19$	$W_{C2/12} = 13$	$W_{C2/13} = 18$	$W_{C2/14} = 19$	$W_{C2/15} = 18$
C3/1	$W_{C3/11} = 21$	$W_{C3/12} = 15$	$W_{C3/13} = 12$	$W_{C3/14} = 12$	$W_{C3/15} = 20$
C4/1	$W_{C4/11} = 15$	$W_{C4/12} = 12$	$W_{C4/13} = 14$	$W_{C4/14} = 17$	$W_{C4/15} = 16$
C5/1	$W_{C5/11} = 12$	$W_{C5/12} = 17$	$W_{C5/13} = 13$	$W_{C5/14} = 15$	$W_{C5/15} = 17$
C6/1	$W_{C6/11} = 17$	$W_{C6/12} = 9$	$W_{C6/13} = 12$	$W_{C6/14} = 8$	$W_{C6/15} = 16$
C7/1	$W_{C7/11} = 21$	$W_{C7/12} = 13$	$W_{C7/13} = 19$	$W_{C7/14} = 19$	$W_{C7/15} = 18$
C8/1	$W_{C8/11} = 21$	$W_{C8/12} = 18$	$W_{C8/13} = 12$	$W_{C8/14} = 16$	$W_{C8/15} = 19$
C9/1	$W_{C9/11} = 15$	$W_{C9/12} = 12$	$W_{C9/13} = 14$	$W_{C9/14} = 17$	$W_{C9/15} = 16$
C10/1	$W_{C10/11} = 23$	$W_{C10/12} = 19$	$W_{C10/13} = 13$	$W_{C10/14} = 15$	$W_{C10/15} = 23$

Other companies can then decide whether the present condition of the knowledge worker as a sales specialist is satisfactory or not.

4.3.1.2 Innovation: Values of the Characteristics of Innovation in a Company: Research Results from Ten Companies

This step involved a survey among selected companies. This was carried out by interviews in the ten companies that conformed to the model of a knowledge worker-oriented company. Based on the research results in the sales area the characteristics of innovation (defined in Sect. 3.2.3) in the ten companies were determined.

where

- X_1—share of new products and technologies in the company's annual sales,
- X_2—number of new products implemented in a given year (for the last 5 years),
- X_3—number of new technologies implemented in a given year (for the last 5 years),
- X_4—number of completed research topics in a given year (for the last 5 years),
- X_5—number of patents in a given year (for the last 5 years),
- X_6—share of spending on research granted during the year to the value of sales,
- X_7—number of employees with science degrees,
- X_8—number of employees with higher education in relation to other staff,
- X_9—number of scientific publications,
- X_{10}—number of awards received in competitions,
- X_{11}—number of sold licenses developed in a given year (for the last 5 years),
- X_{12}—number of implementations of solutions developed in a given year (for the last 5 years), and
- X_{13}—number of purchased and used licenses

Table 4.2 Values of the personnel usefulness function in the sales area in ten companies: the matrix of the personnel usefulness function for five knowledge workers (m = 5) in the sales area (n = 1) in ten companies—workplaces

Company	Workplace in the sale area	W_{1m}	% of max $W_{1m} = 35$	f_1(GK)	f_2(PK)	f_3(A)	f_4(E)	f_5(P)	f_6(C)	f_7(R)
C1	Sales director	25	71	1	5	5	4	0	5	5
C1	Sales specialist	4	12	2	2	0	0	0	0	0
C1	Marketing specialist	12	34	2	4	0	0	0	0	6
C1	Regional assistant	13	37	3	3	2	0	0	1	4
C1	Product manager	16	46	0	3	4	2	0	3	4
C2	Sales director	19	54	2	4	2	2	0	4	5
C2	Sales specialist	13	37	1	4	2	2	0	4	0
C2	Marketing specialist	18	51	3	5	5	3	0	1	1
C2	Regional assistant	19	54	0	2	4	5	0	4	4
C2	Product manager	18	51	3	3	3	5	0	4	0
C3	Sales director	21	60	2	3	5	2	0	4	5
C3	Sales specialist	15	43	2	3	5	1	0	4	0
C3	Marketing specialist	12	34	1	1	5	1	0	4	0
C3	Regional assistant	12	34	1	2	2	0	0	3	4
C3	Product manager	20	57	3	2	5	1	0	4	5
C4	Sales director	15	43	0	4	5	1	0	4	1
C4	Sales specialist	12	34	0	2	5	1	0	4	0
C4	Marketing specialist	14	40	0	3	5	1	0	4	1
C4	Regional assistant	17	49	0	3	5	5	0	4	0
C4	Product manager	16	46	0	2	5	0	0	4	5
C5	Sales director	12	34	0	2	5	0	0	4	1
C5	Sales specialist	17	49	2	3	5	3	0	4	0
C5	Marketing specialist	13	37	2	3	2	1	0	4	1
C5	Regional assistant	15	43	2	4	5	0	0	4	0

(continued)

Table 4.2 (continued)

Company	Workplace in the sale area	W_{1m}	% of max $W_{1m} = 35$	f_1(GK)	f_2(PK)	f_3(A)	f_4(E)	f_5(P)	f_6(C)	f_7(R)
C5	Product manager	17	49	3	1	4	5	0	4	0
C6	Sales director	17	49	1	2	5	4	0	5	0
C6	Sales specialist	9	26	3	2	4	0	0	0	0
C6	Marketing specialist	12	34	2	4	0	0	0	0	6
C6	Regional assistant	8	23	2	3	2	0	0	1	0
C6	Product manager	16	46	0	3	4	2	0	3	4
C7	Sales director	21	60	3	4	2	2	0	4	6
C7	Sales specialist	13	37	1	4	2	2	0	4	0
C7	Marketing specialist	19	54	3	2	5	4	0	1	4
C8	Regional assistant	19	54	3	2	4	2	0	4	4
C8	Product manager	18	51	3	3	3	5	0	4	0
C8	Sales director	21	60	2	3	5	2	0	4	5
C8	Sales specialist	18	51	0	3	5	1	0	4	5
C8	Marketing specialist	12	34	1	1	5	1	0	4	0
C8	Regional assistant	16	46	3	4	2	0	0	3	4
C8	Product manager	19	54	3	2	5	1	0	4	4
C9	Sales director	15	43	0	4	5	1	0	4	1
C9	Sales specialist	12	34	0	2	5	1	0	4	0
C9	Marketing specialist	14	40	0	3	5	1	0	4	1
C9	Regional assistant	17	49	0	3	5	5	0	4	0
C9	Product manager	16	46	0	2	5	0	0	4	5
C10	Sales director	23	66	3	2	5	0	5	4	4
C10	Sales specialist	19	54	2	4	5	3	0	4	1
C10	Marketing specialist	13	37	2	3	2	1	0	4	1
C10	Regional assistant	15	43	2	4	5	0	0	4	0
C10	Product manager	23	66	3	1	4	5	0	4	6

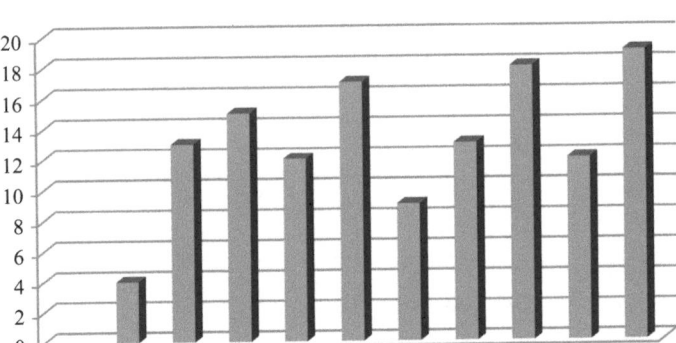

Fig. 4.3 Values of the personnel usefulness function for a sales specialist based on the research results

I will present the possibility of defining a decision-making model for assessing the value of strategic knowledge resources using the GMDH method. This enables values of the personnel usefulness function and those of the characteristics of innovation to be determined. The method involves the following assumptions (Farlow 1984): a precise description of the interdependence between output and input data (selected characteristics of innovation with the value of the personnel usefulness function in the company) and minimum modeling error. By implementing the GMDH algorithm, the best possible polynomial was obtained, which was characterized by the lowest-value criteria for regularity assigned to the pair object.

4.3.1.3 GMDH Algorithm

GMDH is a modeling algorithm based on processing empirical data. It was created by linking elements of the least-squares method and Gödel's theory, and it supplement a procedure for the synthesis of the hierarchical Iwachnienko polynominal (Goldberg 1989; Iwachnienko 1982; Kohonen 1984). GMDH was initially used for the precise prediction of the development of fish populations in rivers and oceans. The algorithm is based on a synthesis of the polynomial model. By integrating structural and parametric optimization concepts, Iwachnienko polynominal, which results from the GMDH procedure, is a model that ensures precise practical application (Iwachnienko 1982). The algorithm eliminates a deductive approach based on engineers' and experts' knowledge. Another important element is the use of polynomial evolution from an elementary structure to an optimized one by selecting various combinations of simple partial models. The features of GMDH include the following (Patalas and Krupa 2007):

- Precise description of relations between input and output data (selected indicators for assessing rationality and effectiveness of investment in

Table 4.3 Values of the characteristics of innovation based on the research results

Company/sale area	X_1	X_2	X_3	X_4	X_5	X_6	X_7	X_8	X_9	X_{10}	X_{11}	X_{12}	X_{13}
C1	1	2	1	1	1	1	5	5	2	1	1	1	5
C2	2	1	1	1	1	1	2	3	1	1	5	5	1
C3	1	1	1	1	1	1	3	5	1	1	1	1	5
C4	1	3	1	2	1	2	5	4	1	3	1	1	5
C5	1	1	1	1	1	1	2	5	1	1	1	1	3
C6	2	1	1	3	1	1	1	4	1	1	5	4	1
C7	2	2	1	5	1	1	2	5	1	1	1	1	2
C8	1	1	1	1	1	1	1	4	1	1	1	1	3
C9	1	4	1	5	1	2	3	5	1	2	1	1	5
C10	1	1	1	4	1	1	2	5	1	1	1	1	3

knowledge, namely investment in human resources and the effects of investment) in the long term,

- Minimizing modeling errors.

The main problem involves a response to the question "Does an assessment of a knowledge worker enhance the innovation level of a company?" (H1); or "Does the selection of a knowledge worker enhance the innovation level of a company?" (H2). I will attempt to find answers for the research hypotheses. In this regard, let us consider the following situation: the problem consisting of determining the value of the personnel usefulness function for the m-th knowledge worker in the sales area and the value of the characteristics of innovation in a company (Tables 4.2 and 4.3).

The decision model is constructed on the basis of the knowledge database. The application of empirical knowledge allows the GMDH algorithm to be used as a modeling tool. Finally, the decision model under examination binds the selected characteristics of innovation in a company with the values of the personnel usefulness function for each m-th knowledge worker. This restriction simplifies the decision-making process and gives it the characteristics of restriction propagation. This means that for some companies, the prediction value for a knowledge worker in terms of innovation level in the company can be made on the basis of previously defined indicators and the company's experience.

A decision-making model for assessing the effectiveness of knowledge worker selection in a company using the GMDH method is presented below.

4.3.2 Sknowinnov Model as a Decision-Making Model for Assessing the Value of Knowledge Workers

The design of this model starts with collecting information about the research subject. The data is obtained by observing the functioning of the subject. Construction of the model encompasses the following:

- Designing the structure of a model for a knowledge worker-oriented company (Sect. 3.2.2)

- Defining the values of strategic knowledge resources (of the knowledge workers) and the values of the qualifying criteria for an innovative company based on an empirical analysis of companies according with the reference model (Tables 4.1 and 4.3)
- Checking the quality of the forecast value of the strategic knowledge resources with the aid of the selected model

Finding knowledge workers who within a defined period of time will guarantee a desired innovation level (as expressed by chosen criteria) is part of the decision-making model. The solution may be presented in the form of the following tasks:

- The possibility for an objective choice (assessment) of an employee, assuming that the following concepts are known:
  - The standard operation areas of the company
  - The structures of business processes related to those areas
  - The values of the strategic knowledge resources
- The possibility of assessing the efficiency of the knowledge worker in terms of the level of innovation in a company

A four-element method for assessing the efficiency of the knowledge worker selection—the Sknowinnov method—has been established (Sect. 4.3.1). The four elements are as follows:

- A model of a company
- The value of the strategic knowledge resources
- The qualifying criteria for an innovative company
- An algorithm that enables the value of the strategic knowledge resources to be connected to the value of the qualifying criteria for an innovative company

The Sknowinnov method was created based on a study of the literature—Chaps. 2 and 3 in this area. It includes methods for assessing the value of IC and methods of employment planning and selection for an innovative company. The method combines available knowledge gained from the literature and the experience—research results of companies that have the potential for innovation. The method allows an assessment to be made regarding the future value of decisions made about selecting knowledge workers so as to increase innovation in a company.

So, a polynomial decision-making model was designed for employee selection by an innovative company. The model compiles all groups of the elements of the Sknowinnov method and consists of the following:

- A base of values for strategic knowledge resources and values for the qualifying criteria for an innovative company (Tables 4.1 and 4.2)
- A GMDH algorithm
- An analyzer of a logical model and an answer generator

A decision-making model for assessing the value of strategic knowledge resources (Sknowinnov model) is built using the GMDH algorithm (Fig. 4.4).

The basic purpose of the GMDH algorithm is to eliminate a deductive approach based on engineers and experts' knowledge. Another important element is the idea of polynomial evolution from an elementary structure to an optimized one by selecting various combinations of simple partial models. In the majority of cases, these are second-degree polynomials with two variables. According to this concept,

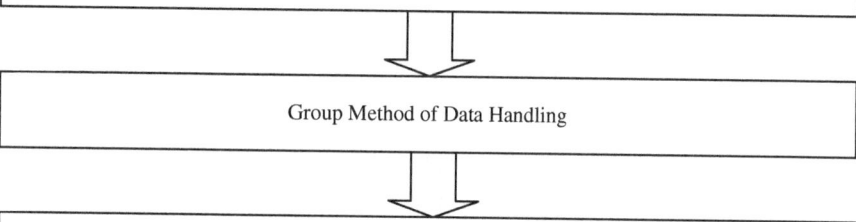

The base value of the personnel usefulness function in companies (data obtained on the basis of empirical research – Table 3.1)
The base value of the determinants values of an innovative company (data obtained on the basis of empirical research – Table 3.3)

Group Method of Data Handling

A decision-making model for an assessment the knowledge worker in the relation to increasing innovation in a company (Sknowinnov model)
- Related indicators: determinants values of an innovative company and values of the personnel usefulness function in companies
- model: $y^* = A_{pq} + B_{pq}x_p + C_{pq}x_q + D_{pq}x_p^2 + E_{pq}x_q^2 + F_{pq}x_px_q$ where:

y – value of the personnel usefulness function for m-the knowledge worker in the company(the base value of the personnel usefulness function)

x_p, x_q – determinants values of an innovative company

A,B,C,D,E,F – estimators value

Fig. 4.4   Structure of the Sknowinnov model

at each iteration arguments supporting the elementary model are polynomial functions that consist of the previous iteration; the degree of the resulting polynomial doubles at each stage of the algorithm. Optimized values of fixed parameters are calculated using the least-squares method. Following publication of the details of the GMDH algorithm, many applications have confirmed its efficiency and broad utilization (Farlow 1984).

Examples of the practical application of the GMDH method based on retrospective data groups are as follows:

- In Britain in 1980–90, a 10-year forecast of inflationary changes was developed for the country using the GMDH method; (the GMDH model for inflation changes was identical with Britain's actual inflation in 1990–2000)
- In the United States in 1990–2000, the GMDH method was used to forecast the development of main economic growth factors
- In Ukraine in 1990–2000, the GMDH method was used to develop a 10-year normative forecast for macroeconomic processes
- The boiler house and steam station of a sugar plant in Lublin, Poland, uses GMDH for precise control of tracking elements. Research into the development and integration (including GMDH) and process-diagnosing techniques (particularly, the regulation valves) in the sugar plant in Lublin was carried out under the project called the Development and Application of Methods for Actuator

Diagnosis in Industrial Control Systems. This was funded by the fifth Framework Programme in 2000–2003, whose project coordinator was Ronald J. Patton, University of Hull, United Kingdom.

The multilevel GMDH algorithm allows the optimalized synthesis of a mathematical model for a given class of regression functions, and it can be used in evaluating criteria and in quality assessment. Both elements of the algorithm are defined arbitrarily by the developer. That is why the modeling must be preceded by an initial identification phase, which allows both defining the choice and the class of the solutions to be carried out. Taking into account the nature of the subject under examination and the tasks that support decision making at the strategic level (in terms of return on investment in knowledge), it can be assumed that the regression function takes the form of two variables. A particle selection of integers is carried out using the regularity criteria.

Developing an object model with the GMDH algorithm is carried out in stages. At every step, the population regression integer is generated. Because the regression function is a function of two variables, the polynomials are assigned to every possible pair of arguments. Their parameters are calculated using the least-squares method, i.e., using the sets of equation formulas. It can be concluded that the GMDH procedure is conditioned by a linear unit independence, which is a guarantee for the solution to be found (Farlow 1984).

Having generated the families of regressive polynomials, a selection is made of those that approximately fit in the interdependence under examination. As a result of calculation assumptions, it is assumed that the number of data (models) in a new population cannot be higher than in the previous one.

For each population of particle solutions, the lowest regularity criteria value is assigned (3). Steps 2 and 3 go through a loop until the value stops decreasing. This results in the optimal model being found—a polynomial of regression for which the criteria has reached the lowest value.

The Sknowinnov model allows a prediction of the characteristics of innovation that will result from hiring a knowledge worker. With this model, defined indicators of innovation in an enterprise with regard to the employment of knowledge workers can be determined. The company is thus in the position of being able to make an objective selection of knowledge workers.

The next chapter presents the decision-making model for an assessment of knowledge workers for increasing innovation in a company (Sknowinnov model). The author's IT tool for supporting decision making at the strategic level with regard to the assessment of knowledge in an innovative company (Appendix 2) will allow research to be conducted.

References

Acedo, F. J., Barroso, C., & Galan, J. L. (2006). The resource-based theory: Dissemination and main trends. *Strategic Management Journal, 27*, 621–636.

Argote, L., & Ingram, P. (2000). Knowledge transfer: A basis for competitive advantage in firms. *Organisational Behavior and Human Decision Processes, 82*(1), 150–169.

Armstrong, M. (2001). *Human resource management.* Kraków: Oficyna Ekonomiczna, Dom Wydawniczy ABC.

Barney, J. B. (1991). The firm resources and sustained competitive advantage. *Journal of Management, 17,* 99–129.

Barney, J. (1995). Looking inside for competitive advantage. *The Academy of Management Executive, 9*(4), 49–61.

Barney, J. B. (2001). Resource-based theories of competitive advantage: A 10-year retrospective on the resource-based view. *Journal of Management, 27,* 643–650.

Barney, J. B., & Zając, E. J. (1994). Competitive organizational behavior: Toward an organizationally-based theory of competitive advantage. *Strategic Management Journal, 15,* 5–9.

Barthelme, F., Ermine, J. L., & Rosenthal-Sabroux, C. (1998). An architecture for knowledge evolution in organisations. *European Journal of Operational Research, 109*(2), 414–427.

Basu, A. (1998). Perspectives on operations research in data and knowledge management. *European Journal of Operational Research, 111*(1), 1–14.

Becker, D. R. (2004). *Ressourcen-Fit bei M&A-Transaktionen: Konzeptionalisierung, Operationlisiernung und Erfolgswirkung auf Basis des Resource-based View.* Wiesbaden: DUV.

Berio, G., & Harzallah, M. (2005). Knowledge management for competence management. *Journal of Universal Knowledge Management, 0*(1), 21–38.

Boos, F., & Jarmai, H. (1994). Kernkompetenzen—gesucht und gefunden. *Harvard Business Manager, 16,* 19–26.

Boxall, P., & Purcell, J. (2000). Strategic human resource management: Where have we come from and where should we be going? *International Journal of Management Reviews, 2,* 183–203.

Carayannis, E. G. (1998). The strategic management of technological learning in project/program management: The role of extranets, intranets and intelligent agents in knowledge generation, diffusion, and leveraging. *Technovation, 18*(11), 697–703.

Chrisman, J. J., Chua, J. H., & Zahra, S. A. (2003). Creating wealth in family firms through managing resources: Comments and extensions. *Entrepreneurship Theory and Practice, 27*(4), 359–365.

Colbert, B. A. (2004). The complex resource-based view: Implication for theory and practice in strategic human resource management. *Academy of Management Review, 29,* 341–358.

Nosal, C. (2002). Time and psychological types—An attempt to reconstruct. In K. Maurin & A. Motycka (Eds.), *About thinking Junga.* Warszawa: Eneteia.

Draganidis, F., & Mentzas, G. (2006). Competency based management: A review of systems and approaches. *Information Management and Computer Security, 14*(1), 51–64.

Drew, S. (1999). Building knowledge management into strategy. Making sense of a new perspective. *Long Range Plan, 32,* 130–136.

Eriksen, B., & Mikkelsen, J. (1996). Competitive advantage and the concept of core competence. In N. J. Foss & C. Knudsen (Eds.), *Towards a competence theory of the firm* (pp. 54–74). New York/London: Routledge.

Farlow, S. J. (1984). *Self-organizing methods in modeling-GMDH type algorithms.* New York: Mersel Dekker.

Freiling, J. (2001). *Resource-based view und ökonomische theorie: grundlagen und positionierung des ressourcenansatzes.* Wiesbaden: Gabler.

Führing, M. (2006). *Risikomanagement und Personal: Management des Fluktuationsrisiko von Schlüsselpersonen aus ressourcenorientierter Perspektive.* Wiesbaden: Springer 11775.

Gajek, L., & Kałuszka, M. (2000). *Methods of statistical inference.* Warszawa: WNT.

Goldberg, D. E. (1989). *The genetic algorithms approach* (pp. 247–253). New York: Plenum Press.

Grant, R. M. (1997). Toward a knowledge-based theory of the firm. *Strategic Management Journal, 17*, 109–122.

Hamel, G., & Prahalad, C. (1994). *Competing for the future*. Boston: Harvard Business School Press.

Hays, S. W., & Kearney, R. C. (2001). Anticipated changes in human resources management: Views from the field. *Public Administration Review, 61*, 309–456.

Helfat, C. E., & Peteraf, M. A. (2003). The dynamic resource based view: Capability lifecycles. *Strategic Management Journal, 24*(10), 997–1010.

Hitt, M. A., Bierman, L., Shimizu, K., & Kochhar, R. (2001). Direct and moderating effects of human capital on strategy and performance in professional service firms: A resource-based perspective. *Academy of Management Journal, 44*(1), 13–28.

Huselid, M. A., Jackson, S. E., & Schuler, R. S. (1997). Technical and strategic human resource management effectiveness as determinants of firms performance. *Academy of Management journal, 40*(1), 171.

Iwachnienko, A. G. (1982). *Induktiwnyj metod samoorganizacji modelej sloznych system po eksperymentalnym danym*. Kijów: Naukowa Dumka.

King, J. (2007). Developing evaluation capacity through process use. In J. B. Cousins (Ed.), *Process use in theory, research, and practice: New directions for evaluation* (p. 116). San Francisco: Jossey-Bass.

Kohonen, T. (1984). *Self-organization and associative memory*. Berlin: Springer.

Kosieradzka, A., Lis, S. (2000). Produktywność (Productivity). Warszawa.

Kostera, M. (2000). *Zarządzanie personelem (Personnel management)*. Warszawa: PWE.

Krämer, C., Ringling, S., & Yang, S. (2005). *Mastering HR management with SAP. The complete guide to SAP HR*. Bonn: Galileo Press.

Król, H., & Ludwiczyński, A. (2007). *Zarządzanie zasobami ludzkimi (Human resources management)*. Warszawa: PWN.

Lado, A. A., & Wilson, M. C. (1994). Human resource system and sustained competitive advantage: A competency-based perspective. *The Academy of Management Review, 19*(4), 699.

Lichtarski, J. (2000). Personnel function and personnel management. In T. Listwan (Ed.), *Personnel management*. Wrocław: Economical University.

Maier, R. (2002). *Knowledge management systems: Information and communication technologies for knowledge management*. Berlin: Springer.

Makadok, R. (2001). Toward a synthesis of the resource-based and dynamic-capability view of rent creation. *Strategic Management Journal, 22*, 387–401.

McGrath, R., & MacMillan, I. (2000). *The entrepreneurial mindset*. Boston: Harvard Business School Press.

McKenna, E., & Beech, N. (1997). *Human resource management*. Warszawa: Gebethner&S-ka.

Nolte, H., Bergmann, R. (1998). Ein Grundmodell des ressourcenorientierten Ansatzes der Unternehmens-führung. In H. Nolte (Hrsg.): Aspekte ressourcenorientierter Unternehmensführung (S. 1–27). Hampp: Mün-chen – Mering.

Nordhaug, O. (1993). *Human capital in organizations*. Oslo: Scandinavian University Press.

Patalas, J., & Krupa, T. (2007). The prediction value of criteria of ERP system efficiency in small and medium size enterprises (SMES). In J. Jakubowski & B. Franczyk (Eds.), *Production engineering: Computer science driven production engineering*. University of Zielona Góra.

Patalas-Maliszewska, J. (2009). The concept of system supporting decision making enabling to asses and forecast of knowledge in SMEs—Research results. *Applied Computer Science, 5*(2), 27–41.

Patalas-Maliszewska, J. (2011). The personnel usefulness function—the method for planning and selection of personnel in SME. *Management, 15*(2), 132–143.

Patalas-Maliszewska, J., & Hochmeister, M. (2011). Modeling strategic-knowledge-resource management based on individual competencies in SMEs. *Contemporary Economics, 5*, 72–79.

Patalas-Maliszewska, J., & Werthner, H. (2010). Methodology of knowledge value assessment in an enterprise of SME sector. *Management and Production Engineering Review, 1*(1), 21–28.

Pawlak, Z. (2003). *Personnel business function—Processes and procedures for staff.* Warszawa: Poltext.

Penner-Hahn, J., & Shaver, J. M. (2005). Does international research and development increase patent output? An analysis of Japanese pharmaceutical firms. *Strategic Management Journal, 26*(2), 121–140.

Penrose, E. T. (1959). *The theory of the growth of the firm.* New York: Wiley.

Perry, E. L., Kulik, C. T., & Bourhis, A. C. (1996). Moderating effects of personal and contextual factors in age discrimination. *Journal of Applied Psychology, 81*, 628–647.

Pfeffer, J., & Salancik, G. (1978). *The external control of organizations: A resource-dependence perspective.* New York: Harper-Rowe.

Prezewowsky, M. (2007). Demografischer Wandel und Personalmanagement: Herausforderungen und Handlungsalternativen vor dem Hintergrund der Bevölkerungsentwicklung. Wiesbaden.

Priem, R. L., & Butler, J. E. (2001). Is the resource-based view a useful perspective for strategic management research? *Academy of Management Review, 26*, 41–56.

Purser, R. E., & Pasmore, W. A. (1992). *Organizing for learning. Research in organization or change and development* (pp. 37–114). London: JAI Press.

Ramos-Rodriguez, A. R., & Ruiz-Navarro, J. (2004). Changes in the intellectual structure of strategic management research: A bibliometric study of the strategic management journal, 1980–2000. *Strategic Management Journal, 25*(10), 981–1004.

Sekuła, Z. (2001). Planowanie personelu (Personnel planning). Kraków: Economical University.

Sirmon, D., & Hitt, M. A. (2003). Managing resources: Linking unique resources, management and wealth creation in family firms. *Entrepreneurship Theory and Practice, 27*, 339–358.

Smart, D. L., & Wolfe, R. A. (2000). Examining sustainable competitive advantage in intercollegiate athletics: A resource-based view. *Journal of Sport Management, 14*, 133–153.

Studer, R., Benjamins, V. R., & Fensel, D. (1998). Knowledge engineering: Principles and methods. *Data Knowledge Engineering, 25*(1–2), 161–197.

Szałkowski, A. (Ed.). (2002). Personel development. Kraków: Economical University.

Teece, D. J., Pisano, G., & Shuen, A. (1997). Dynamic capabilities and strategic management. *Strategic Management Journal, 18*(7), 509–533.

Wernerfelt, B. (1984). A resource-based view of the firm. *Strategic Management Journal, 5*, 171–180.

Wright, P. M., Dunford, B. B., & Snell, S. A. (2001). Human resources and the resource based view of the firm. *Journal of Management, 18*, 207–229.

Examples of Applications of the Sknowinnov Model in Creating an Innovative Company

5

The success of a company lies more in its IC than in its physical assets. The capacity to manage knowledge and convert it into useful products and services is fast becoming the current primary executive skill. As a result, there has been a flurry of interest in IC, creativity, innovation, and learning within an organization. However, surprisingly little attention has been given to the management of dependence on the value of IC and innovation in a company.

The Sknowinnov method (Chap. 4) allows the construction of a decision model that involves all the elements of Sknowinnov, including an assessment of the method's implementation efficiency. The modeling object consists of a pair of values: the values of the personnel usefulness function for the m-th knowledge worker and the values of innovation characteristics. The application of the Sknowinnov model makes it possible to forecast the value of knowledge workers. The solution, defined in terms of predictive indicators for the efficiency in knowledge worker selection, will be shown using the consulting software. Only the employment of appropriate knowledge workers can guarantee a company's enduring competitive edge in the market.

This chapter presents my system for assessing knowledge workers in relation to increasing innovation in a company (Sknowinnov system). Through the research studies, I will show how forecasting the values of strategic knowledge resources (values of the personnel usefulness function for the m-th knowledge worker) are carried out. Two medium-sized companies that fulfill the qualifying criteria of innovative companies, were chosen as test subjects for the effectiveness of the Sknowinnov method. The research questions included the following. Is it possible to forecast the values of the personnel usefulness function for the m-th knowledge worker when given the values of the characteristics of innovation in a company? Is it possible to identify knowledge workers who can become innovative workers?

J. Patalas-Maliszewska, *Managing Knowledge Workers*, Management for Professionals,
DOI 10.1007/978-3-642-36600-0_5, © Springer-Verlag Berlin Heidelberg 2013

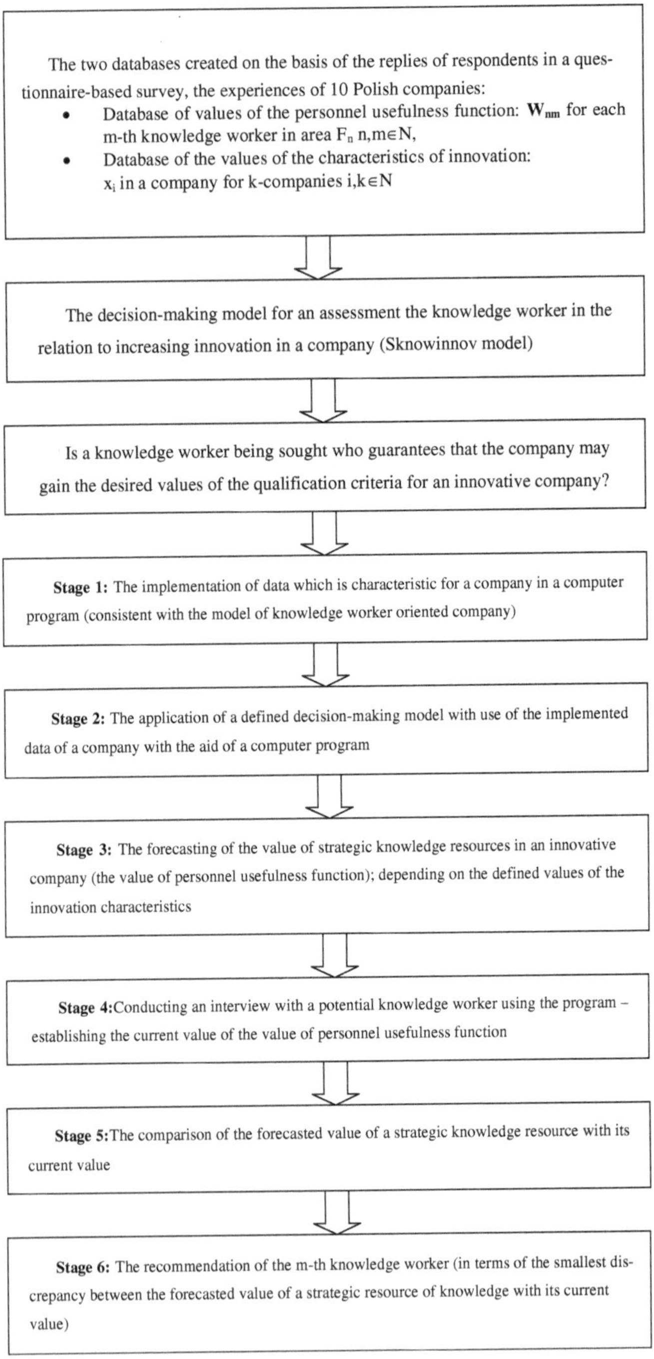

The two databases created on the basis of the replies of respondents in a questionnaire-based survey, the experiences of 10 Polish companies:
- Database of values of the personnel usefulness function: W_{nm} for each m-th knowledge worker in area F_n $n,m \in N$,
- Database of the values of the characteristics of innovation: x_i in a company for k-companies $i,k \in N$

The decision-making model for an assessment the knowledge worker in the relation to increasing innovation in a company (Sknowinnov model)

Is a knowledge worker being sought who guarantees that the company may gain the desired values of the qualification criteria for an innovative company?

Stage 1: The implementation of data which is characteristic for a company in a computer program (consistent with the model of knowledge worker oriented company)

Stage 2: The application of a defined decision-making model with use of the implemented data of a company with the aid of a computer program

Stage 3: The forecasting of the value of strategic knowledge resources in an innovative company (the value of personnel usefulness function); depending on the defined values of the innovation characteristics

Stage 4: Conducting an interview with a potential knowledge worker using the program – establishing the current value of the value of personnel usefulness function

Stage 5: The comparison of the forecasted value of a strategic knowledge resource with its current value

Stage 6: The recommendation of the m-th knowledge worker (in terms of the smallest discrepancy between the forecasted value of a strategic resource of knowledge with its current value)

Fig. 5.1 The decision-making situation in which an innovative company is considering the employment of a new m-th knowledge worker

5.1 Sknowinnov System

5.1.1 Selection of Appropriate Knowledge Workers

The decision regarding the selection of appropriate employees requires that the company management assess the efficiency of the investment. The application of this model allows a forecast to be made about the value of the strategic knowledge resources within a given organization (Patalas-Maliszewska 2009). The decision-making situation, in which an innovative company is considering the employment of the m-th knowledge worker, is presented in Fig. 5.1.

The decision-making situation of the company has been presented; this determines whether the new knowledge worker should be employed in sales. In addition, I will describe the example of company A2, which is looking for an employee to fill the position of regional assistant. That company expects to retain its current level of innovation.

The decision situation is as follows.

Stage 1. Using the computer-based Sknowinnov system, it is possible to check whether the company complies with the specified reference model. A potential new employee selects actions that will be performed in the company. The developed reference model will help companies determine the work place for a new employee.

Stage 2. A tool in the Sknowinnov method supports decision making at the strategic level for assessing knowledge in an innovative company. The following information is produced:

- For m_4—regional assistant:

$$m_4{}^* = -0,6490 + 3,4592X_7 - 2,2539X_{13} - 2,0984X_7{}^2 - 1,7486X_{13}{}^2 + 3,8323X_7X_{13},$$

where

X_7—number of employees with science degrees,
X_{13}—number of purchased and used licenses.

Stage 3. For a new potential knowledge worker as a regional assistant, by using the decision model we obtain the following forecast of the personnel usefulness function. This is the company's request for the sample of A2's values for knowledge worker:

$$m_4{}^* = -0,6490 + 3,4592X_7 - 2,2539X_{13} - 2,0984X_7{}^2 - 1,7486X_{13}{}^2 + 3,8323X_7X_{13},$$

where

X$_7$—number of employees with scientific degrees, and
X$_{13}$—number of purchased and used licenses.

Stage 4. Using the Sknowinnov system, the actual value of the personnel usefulness function for a new employee is checked (see Appendix 1).

Stage 5. We then compare the actual value of the personnel usefulness function
with the expected value for the new employee. If these values are similar, it is
assumed that the employment of the employee will allow the current level of
innovation to be maintained within the company.
The actual value of the function: $Wm_4 = 19$
The forecast value of the function:

$$Wm_4{}^* = -0,6490 + 3,4592X_7 - 2,2539X_{13} + 2,0984X_7{}^2 - 1,7486X_{13}{}^2$$
$$+ 3,8323X_7X_{13}$$
$$= 19,6231$$

for X$_7$—number of employees with science degrees, $X_7 = 2$,
X$_{13}$—number of purchased and used licenses, $X_{13} = 1$.
The company may decide to recruit new employees for the position of regional
assistant. This is because the predicted value of the personnel usefulness function
for the new employee is in line with the actual value of the function, which would
allow the company to maintain a certain level of innovation.
The resulting decision-making models may take different forms if changes are
made to the databases (database of values for the personnel usefulness function,
database of values for the characteristics of innovation). The larger the database is
(based on experiments and research results), the more accurate the defined decision-
making models will be.
The following section presents the decision-making situation in which an innovative company is considering the employment of a new m-th knowledge worker.

5.1.2 Designing a Decision-Making Model for Assessing the Value of a Knowledge Worker

Based on information found in the database for the values of strategic knowledge
resources and the qualification criteria for an innovative company, the variants of
the GMDH algorithm available in the computer program are examined.
Because of the possibility of using the GMDH algorithm only for nonsingular
matrices, the decision-making model with the following characteristics of
innovation is obtained:
* X$_2$—number of new products implemented in a given year (for the last 5 years),
* X$_4$—number of completed research topics in a given year (for the last 5 years),
* X$_7$—number of employees with science degrees,

- X_8—number of employees with higher education in relation to other staff, and
- X_{13}—number of purchased and used licenses.

For m_1—sales director:

The GMDH algorithm uses the best possible polynomial, which is characterized by the lowest-value criteria for regularity assigned to the pair object (the values of the characteristics of innovation in a company and the values of the personnel usefulness function for the sales area). The algorithm evolution process is completed on the second iteration. It should be noted that the second-degree polynomial is obtained as a result of implementing the defined database. Thus, it can be different from the value of characteristics of innovation.

In this way, the best polynomial is chosen, which is the one with the smallest error of modeling.

$$m_1{}^* = 20,07759 + 0,6842X_2 - 2,1282X_4 + 0,0909X_2{}^2 + 0,1610X_4{}^2 \\ - 0,1818X_2X_4,$$

where

X_2—number of new products implemented in a given year (for the last 5 years), and

X_4—number of completed research topics in a given year (for the last 5 years).

For m_2—sales specialist:

In this way, the best polynomial is chosen, which is the one with the smallest error of modeling.

$$m_2{}^* = -34,1402 + 10,12823X_4 - 4,3094X_{13} + 0,0861X_4{}^2 + 0,8112X_{13}{}^2 \\ - 1,0611X_4X_{13},$$

where

X_4—number of completed research topics in a given year (for the last 5 years), X_{13}—number of purchased and used licenses.

For m_3—marketing specialist:

In this way, the best polynomial is chosen, which is the one with the smallest error of modeling.

$$m_3{}^* = -1,0920 + 6,0274X_2 - 5,3324X_4 + 0,3174X_2{}^2 + 0,5490X_4{}^2 \\ - 0,8606X_2X_4,$$

where

X_2—number of new products implemented in a given year (for the last 5 years), and

X_4—number of completed research topics in a given year (for the last 5 years).

For m_4—regional assistant:

In this way, the best polynomial is chosen, which is the one with the smallest error of modeling.

$$m_4{}^* = -0,6490 + 3,4592X_7 - 2,2539X_{13} + 2,0984X_7{}^2 - 1,7486X_{13}{}^2$$
$$+ 3,8323X_7X_{13},$$

where
X$_7$—number of employees with science degrees,
X$_{13}$—number of purchased and used licenses.
For m$_5$—product manager:
In this way, the best polynomial is chosen, which is the one with the smallest error of modeling.

$$m_5{}^* = -10,0552 + 3,4124X_4 - 0,2434X_8 - 0,2298X_4{}^2 - 0,0193X_8{}^2$$
$$+ 0,1261X_4X_8,$$

where
X$_4$—number of employees with science degrees,
X$_8$—number of purchased and used licenses.
Polynomial models of decision making (Figs. 5.2, 5.3, 5.4, 5.5, 5.6, 5.7, 5.8, 5.9, 5.10, 5.11, 5.12, 5.13, 5.14, 5.15, 5.16, 5.17, 5.18, 5.19, 5.20, 5.21, 5.22, 5.23, 5.24, 5.25, 5.26, 5.27, 5.28, 5.29, and 5.30) are constructed from the four groups in the Sknowinnov method (Chap. 4). The Sknowinnov model allows the determination of the value of the personnel usefulness function for a new employee, including the value of innovation characteristics. Based on the projected value of these indicators, the company management can decide on the selection of a new knowledge worker (Fig. 5.1).

5.2   Case Studies Using the Sknowinnov System

5.2.1   Selection of Appropriate Knowledge Workers in an IT Company

The decision about selection appropriate knowledge workers requires the company management to assess the efficiency of the investment. The application of the Sknowinnov model allows a forecast to be made about the value of knowledge workers. The decision-making situation for a company considering the employment of the m-th knowledge worker is presented below.

To illustrate the use of the Sknowinnov model, I will consider an IT company that provides services in the form of projects for both organizations and individual customers (Fig. 5.31). The company decides that it needs to find a new employee to fill the position of sales specialist. It is assumed that in hiring the new employee, the company wishes to maintain its level of innovation.

The Sknowinnov model was used to assess the following employment decisions:

Fig. 5.2 Example of the Sknowinnov system in use

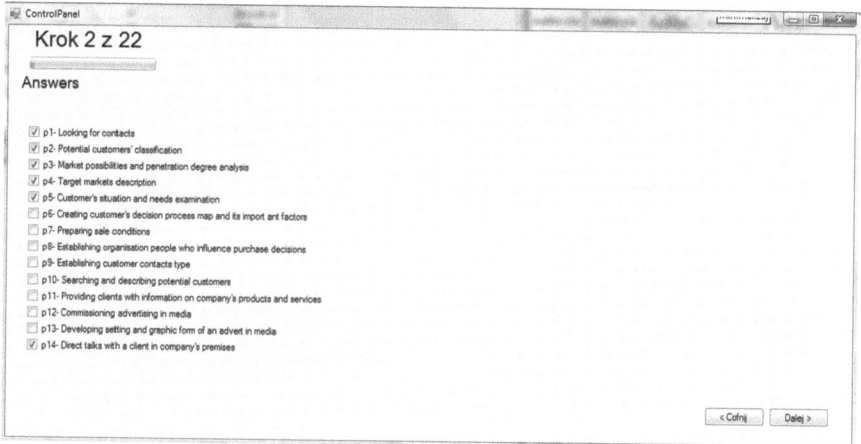

Fig. 5.3 Example of the Sknowinnov system in use

$$Wm_{*2} = -34,14 + 10,13x_4 - 4,31x_{13} + 0,09x_4{}^2 + 0,811x_{13}{}^2$$
$$+ 1,06x_4x_{13,}\text{where}$$

Wm^*_2—value of the personnel usefulness function for the sales specialist, x_4—number of completed research topics in a given year (for the last 5 years—at the IT company this was four research topics), x_{13}—number of purchased and used licenses (at the IT company this was three licenses).

The model compiles all groups of the elements of the Sknowinnov method. A decision-making model for a selection of the knowledge (Sknowinnov model) was built for each of five knowledge workers based on empirical research and using

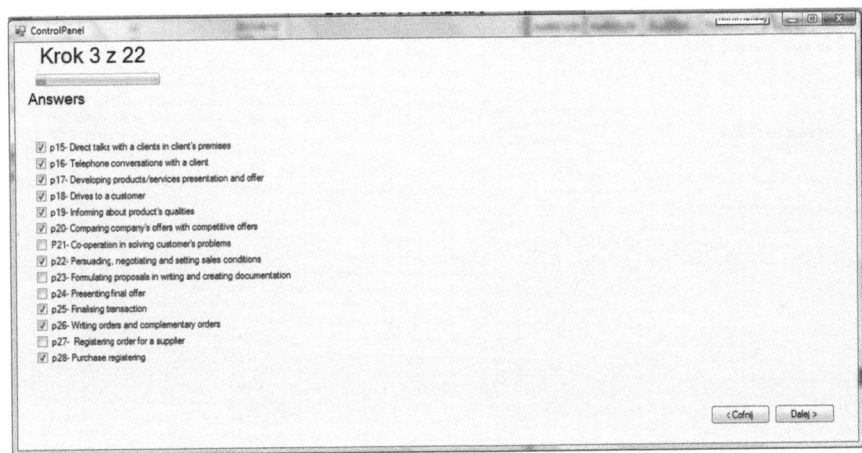

Fig. 5.4 Example of the Sknowinnov system in use

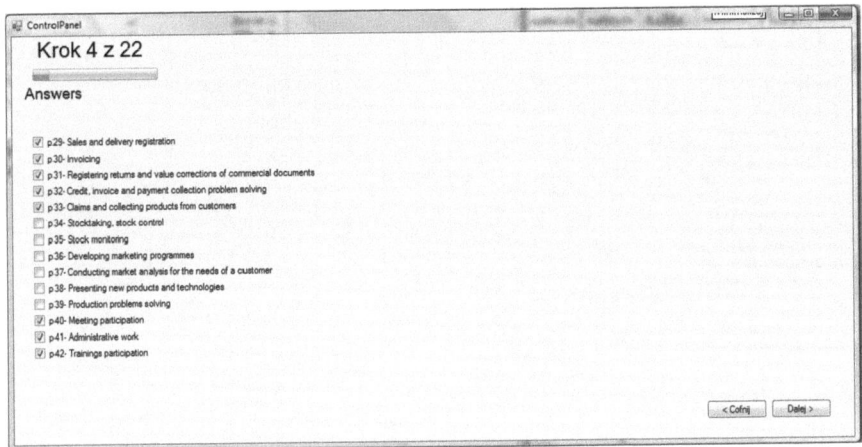

Fig. 5.5 Example of the Sknowinnov system in use

GMDH. It allows a forecast to be made about the future value of the decision about the selecting an employee to increase a company's innovation capacity.

With the Sknowinnov model, the estimated value of the personnel usefulness function (Wm^*_2) for the new knowledge worker to fill the position of sales specialist was determined as: $Wm^*_2 = 14{,}86$. The prospective knowledge worker then completed the test for the Sknowinnov system to obtain the value of the personnel usefulness function (Wm_2). The actual value of the personnel usefulness function for the prospective employee was $Wm_2 = 11$. Examples of using the Sknowinnov system to obtain actual values for the personnel usefulness function Wm_2 are presented in Figs. 5.2, 5.3, 5.4, 5.5, 5.6, 5.7, 5.8, 5.9, 5.10, 5.11, 5.12, 5.13,

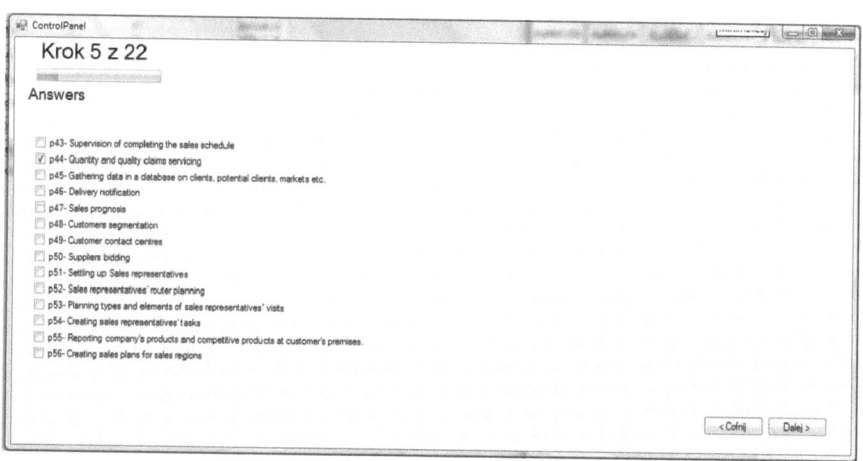

Fig. 5.6 Example of the Sknowinnov system in use

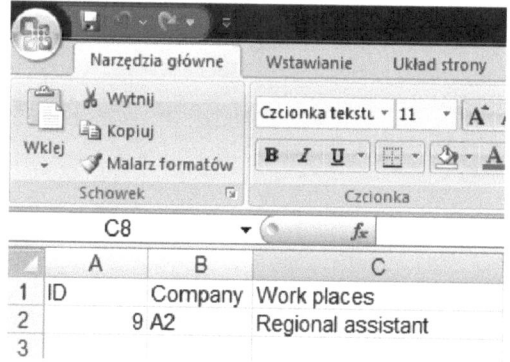

Fig. 5.7 Example of the Sknowinnov system in use

5.14, 5.15, 5.16, 5.17, 5.18, 5.19, 5.20, 5.21, 5.22, 5.23, 5.24, 5.25, 5.26, 5.27, 5.28, and 5.29. The managing director of the IT company should not select this person since his personnel usefulness function was unsatisfactory compared with the projected value of this function at a given level of innovation.

In addition to being a calculation of the profitability of investment, this approach would appear to be an excellent tool for an "economic" quantitative knowledge analysis. The Sknowinnov model (based on collected data) connects selected determinants described for an innovative company with the value of the personnel usefulness function. It thus allows an assessment of the rationality of hiring knowledge workers and their potential effectiveness. In consequence, this model permits a quantitative evaluation of knowledge workers in a company to be made.

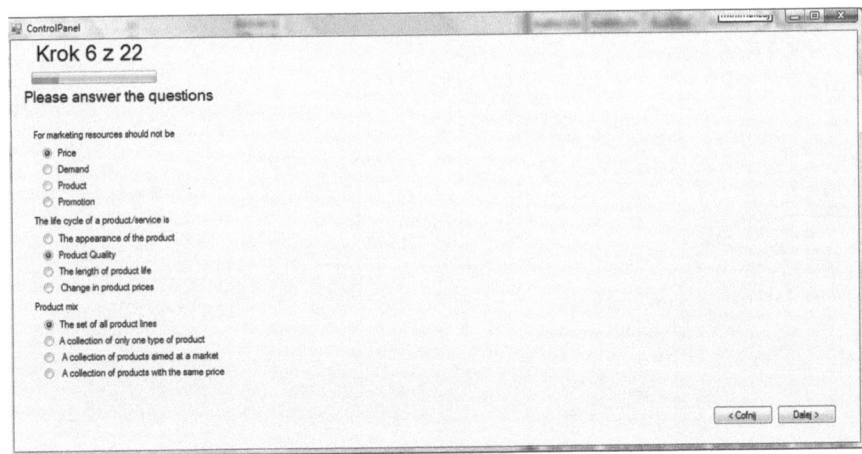

Fig. 5.8 Example of the Sknowinnov system in use

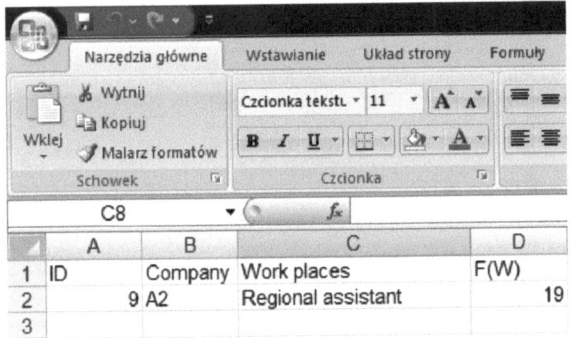

Fig. 5.9 Example of the Sknowinnov system in use

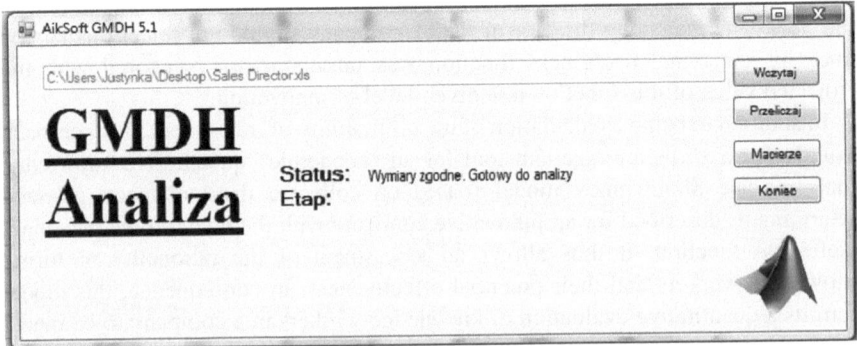

Fig. 5.10 Example of the Sknowinnov system in use

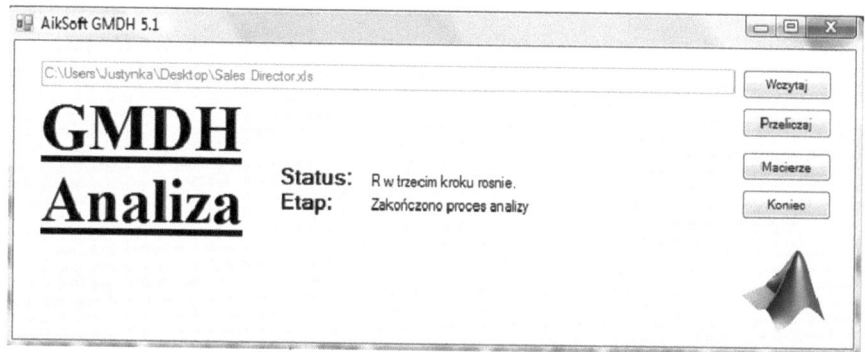

Fig. 5.11 Example of the Sknowinnov system in use

A	B	C	D	E	F	G	H	I	J	K
25,19151	25,0134	24,93441	25,02932	22,72973	24,32886	24,96092	24,90331	25,0116	24,89318	
17,44057	18,24088	17,84917	18,25415	18,28863	17,71991	18,29876	18,98104	18,41218	19,69222	
19,32099	20,99864	21,42723	21,14168	18,09536	18,04447	17,81062	18,53474	20,27858	18,86905	
15,08672	14,92262	14,82706	14,91692	15,57437	16,52772	15,25381	15,20494	15,00668	15,40242	
17,44057	18,14621	17,84917	18,11269	18,09536	17,71991	18,09353	18,34839	18,74861	18,13203	
18,03857	18,73851	17,99204	18,79427	17,76836	17,77755	17,22448	19,20777	18,41218	17,92625	
21,9257	21,03591	20,88481	20,82892	23,37237	22,39608	21,73151	21,06046	21,05622	21,36638	
17,89258	18,73851	20,28208	18,79427	18,28863	17,72622	18,29876	19,75324	18,41218	20,30814	
14,36927	15,0191	15,32676	15,0151	14,30498	14,20224	14,83318	14,83788	14,91316	14,36617	
22,29352	18,14621	17,62727	18,11269	22,48223	22,55705	22,49444	18,16823	18,74861	18,04416	
0,112845	0,137212	0,133423	0,137107	0,133082	0,126961	0,122706	0,143136	0,140244	0,136399	

A1 = 25,1915114088143

Fig. 5.12 Example of the Sknowinnov system in use

A	B	C	D	E	F	G	H	I	J	K
20,07759	-4,52199	22,85335	4,365588	15,8021	21,72464	-61,6115	3,897236	-142,388	-181,101	
0,684216	0,616054	4,197515	7,073833	-1,48599	0,831755	5,372982	6,871927	46,64047	46,95533	
-2,1282	0,958127	-5,44727	-6,53432	0,531593	-2,32719	1,739868	-6,18252	-28,5357	-27,4201	
0,090988	0,209777	0,462675	0,0498	0,130076	0,105208	0,096058	0,672617	0,109944	0,278797	
0,161037	0,178094	0,655588	0,392576	0,076099	0,179806	0,191339	1,013478	2,098081	2,324989	
-0,18179	-0,40608	-1,06519	-0,43061	-0,14893	-0,21663	-0,44026	-1,68232	-2,71548	-3,07908	
1;2	1;3	1;4	1;5	2;3	2;4	2;5	3;4	3;5	4;5	

A1 = 20,0775864138176

Fig. 5.13 Example of the Sknowinnov system in use

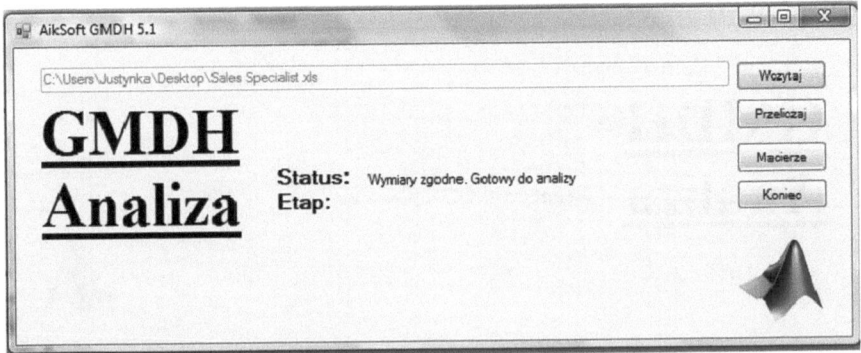

Fig. 5.14 Example of the Sknowinnov system in use

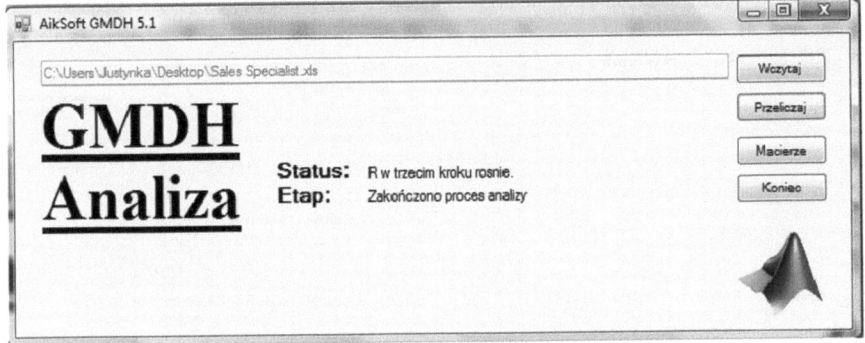

Fig. 5.15 Example of the Sknowinnov system in use

5.2.2   Selection of Appropriate Knowledge Workers by a Service Company

The main purpose of the next experiment was to determine and compare the forecasts of the value of the personnel usefulness function for a new m-th knowledge worker; this depends on the defined values of the characteristics of innovation. The object of this experiment for examining the effectiveness of the Sknowinnov method consists of two features—a service company faced with choosing a new employee and the defined innovation characteristics.

A service company decided that it needed to find a new employee to fill the position of sales specialist. It was assumed that following the hiring of the new employee, the company would maintain its current level of innovation. The Sknowinnov model was used to assess the employment decisions:

$$Wm*_{12} = -34,14 + 10,13x_4 - 4,31x_{13} + 0,09x_4{}^2 + 0,811x_{13}{}^2 + 1,06x_4x_{13}, \text{where:}$$

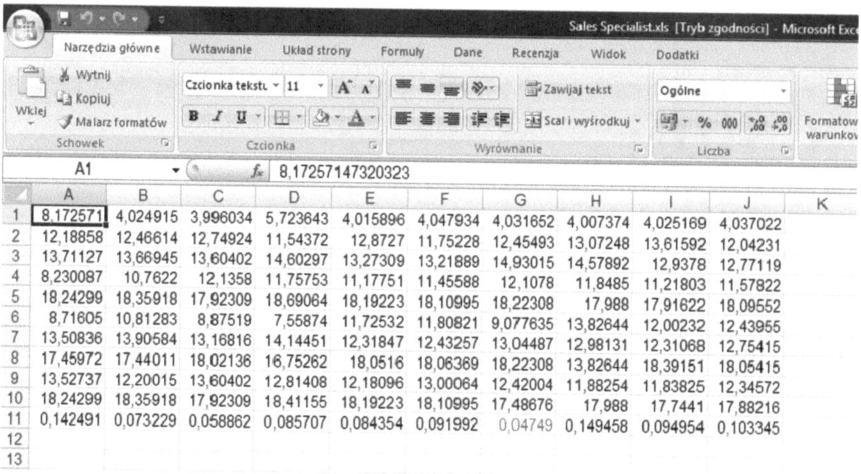

	A	B	C	D	E	F	G	H	I	J	K
1	8,172571	4,024915	3,996034	5,723643	4,015896	4,047934	4,031652	4,007374	4,025169	4,037022	
2	12,18858	12,46614	12,74924	11,54372	12,8727	11,75228	12,45493	13,07248	13,61592	12,04231	
3	13,71127	13,66945	13,60402	14,60297	13,27309	13,21889	14,93015	14,57892	12,9378	12,77119	
4	8,230087	10,7622	12,1358	11,75753	11,17751	11,45588	12,1078	11,8485	11,21803	11,57822	
5	18,24299	18,35918	17,92309	18,69064	18,19223	18,10995	18,22308	17,988	17,91622	18,09552	
6	8,71605	10,81283	8,87519	7,55874	11,72532	11,80821	9,077635	13,82644	12,00232	12,43955	
7	13,50836	13,90584	13,16816	14,14451	12,31847	12,43257	13,04487	12,98131	12,31068	12,75415	
8	17,45972	17,44011	18,02136	16,75262	18,0516	18,06369	18,22308	13,82644	18,39151	18,05415	
9	13,52737	12,20015	13,60402	12,81408	12,18096	13,00064	12,42004	11,88254	11,83825	12,34572	
10	18,24299	18,35918	17,92309	18,41155	18,19223	18,10995	17,48676	17,988	17,7441	17,88216	
11	0,142491	0,073229	0,058862	0,085707	0,084354	0,091992	0,04749	0,149458	0,094954	0,103345	
12											
13											

Fig. 5.16 Example of the Sknowinnov system in use

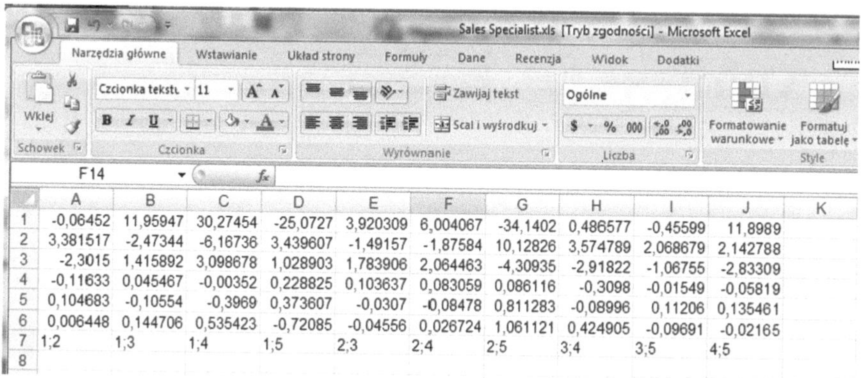

	A	B	C	D	E	F	G	H	I	J	K
1	-0,06452	11,95947	30,27454	-25,0727	3,920309	6,004067	-34,1402	0,486577	-0,45599	11,8989	
2	3,381517	-2,47344	-6,16736	3,439607	-1,49157	-1,87584	10,12826	3,574789	2,068679	2,142788	
3	-2,3015	1,415892	3,098678	1,028903	1,783906	2,064463	-4,30935	-2,91822	-1,06755	-2,83309	
4	-0,11633	0,045467	-0,00352	0,228825	0,103637	0,083059	0,086116	-0,3098	-0,01549	-0,05819	
5	0,104683	-0,10554	-0,3969	0,373607	-0,0307	-0,08478	0,811283	-0,08996	0,11206	0,135461	
6	0,006448	0,144706	0,535423	-0,72085	-0,04556	0,026724	1,061121	0,424905	-0,09691	-0,02165	
7	1;2	1;3	1;4	1;5	2;3	2;4	2;5	3;4	3;5	4;5	
8											

Fig. 5.17 Example of the Sknowinnov system in use

where Wm^*_2—value of the personnel usefulness function for the sales specialist, X_4—number of completed research topics in a given year (for the last 5 years—at the this was 5 completed research topics), X_{13}—number of purchased and used licenses (at the company this was one license).

The estimated value of the personnel usefulness function (Wm_{12}) for the new employee to fill the sales specialist position was $W_{12}^* = 20{,}46$. The prospective employee then completed the test to obtain the value of the personnel usefulness function (Wm2) according to the employee personnel evaluation sheet (described in detail in Appendix 2). The actual value of the personnel usefulness function for the prospective employee was $W_{12} = 21$ (Figs. 5.32, 5.33, and 5.34).

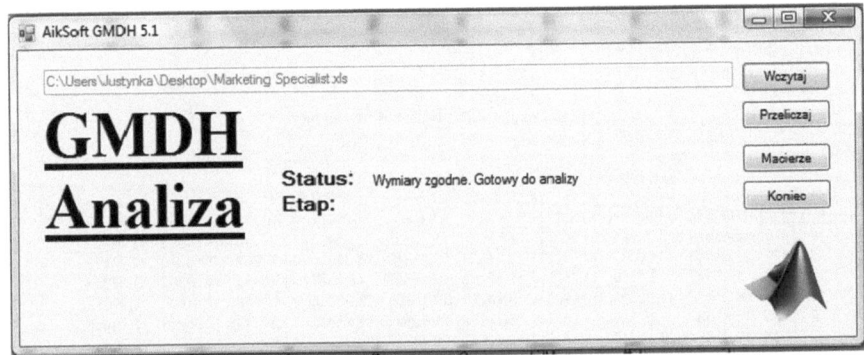

Fig. 5.18 Example of the Sknowinnov system in use

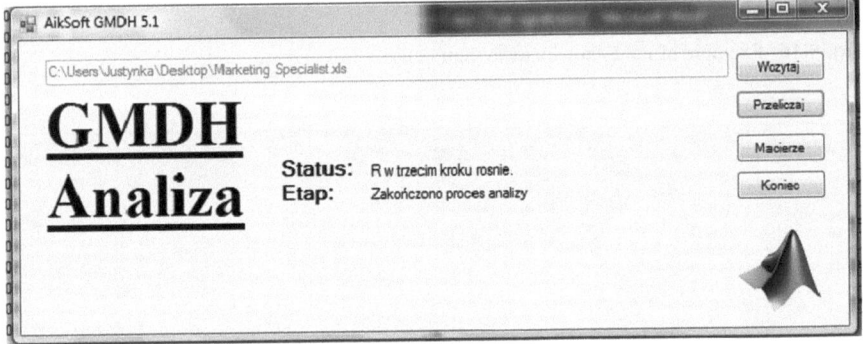

Fig. 5.19 Example of the Sknowinnov system in use

	A	B	C	D	E	F	G	H	I	J	K
1	11,99771	12,00178	12,00119	12,00134	12,00133	12,0023	12,00223	13,94699	12,00076	12,00149	
2	17,99912	18,00001	18,0001	17,99999	18,00001	18,00002	18,0004	23,02305	18	18,00001	
3	12,00215	11,99961	12,00053	12,00101	12,00226	12,00093	12,00155	13,9481	12,00314	12,00218	
4	13,99909	13,99918	13,99765	13,99903	13,99916	13,99936	14,00027	16,77404	13,99971	14,00101	
5	12,99189	12,9917	12,99216	12,99158	12,99154	12,99136	12,99161	15,32414	12,99154	12,99114	
6	11,99835	12,00005	11,99988	11,99953	11,99894	11,99946	11,99948	13,94316	11,9986	11,99871	
7	18,99898	19,00001	19,00006	19,00002	18,99998	19,00001	19,00043	24,72335	19	19	
8	11,99982	11,99862	11,9985	11,99827	11,99749	11,9974	11,99759	13,94176	11,99759	11,99769	
9	13,99942	14,00074	14,00219	14,00101	14,00068	14,00055	14,00015	16,77597	14,00021	13,99888	
10	13,00728	13,00831	13,00816	13,00827	13,00855	13,00869	13,00884	15,3482	13,00845	13,0089	
11	0,00026	0,000269	0,000267	0,000272	0,000284	0,000287	0,000288	0,22348	0,000285	0,000296	
12											

Fig. 5.20 Example of the Sknowinnov system in use

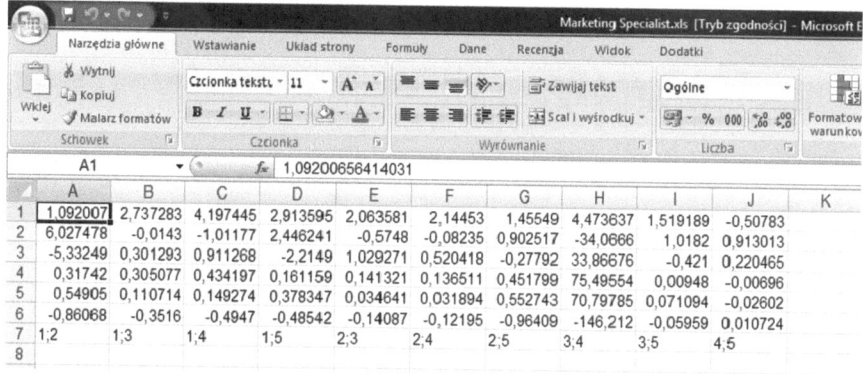

Fig. 5.21 Example of the Sknowinnov system in use

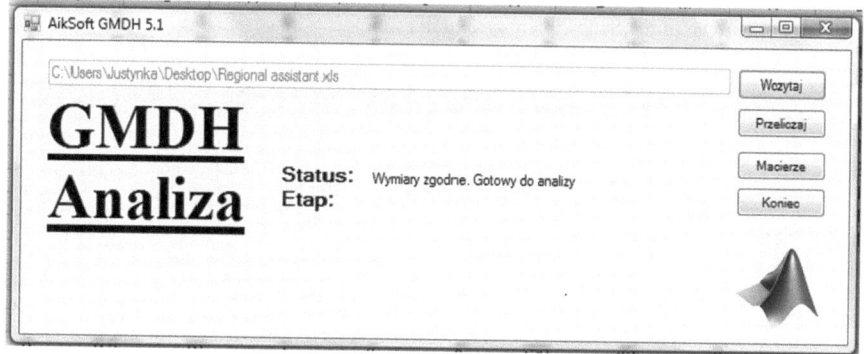

Fig. 5.22 Example of the Sknowinnov system in use

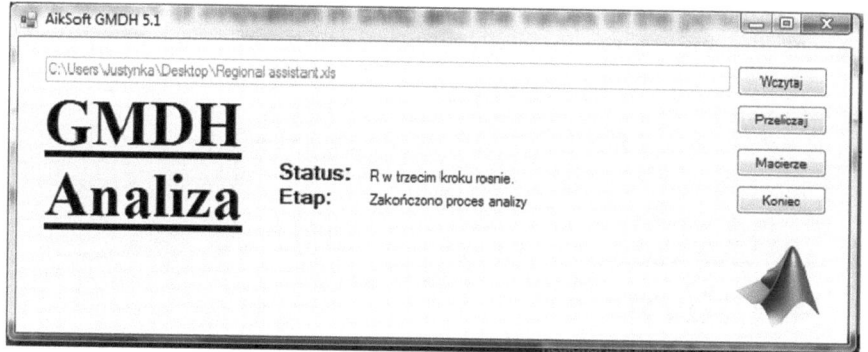

Fig. 5.23 Example of the Sknowinnov system in use

Regional assistant.xls [Tryb zgodności] - Microsoft Ex

A1 f_x 7,47203085178353

	A	B	C	D	E	F	G	H	I	J	K
1	7,472031	10,24824	13,22243	13,00104	15,11097	13,97233	13,00324	-121,859	13,00157	13,0019	
2	7,281997	13,17389	19,47241	19,00111	23,46784	21,04349	19,00185	-262,56	18,99965	18,99982	
3	7,283056	9,653919	12,18911	11,99957	13,79669	12,82771	11,99982	-103,353	11,99916	11,99902	
4	7,594832	12,32341	17,38154	17,00311	20,59118	18,6477	17,00478	-210,143	17,00286	17,00303	
5	7,658654	11,34701	15,29413	14,99856	17,79858	16,28346	14,99973	-163,076	14,99768	14,99801	
6	5,893028	6,954373	8,084238	8,00009	8,802535	8,372254	8,000529	-44,2577	8,000071	8,000102	
7	7,282526	13,17268	19,47305	18,99975	23,47011	21,04684	19,00376	-262,677	19,00064	19,00076	
8	7,658406	11,84843	16,33342	15,99772	19,18081	17,45812	16,00015	-185,849	15,99847	15,99807	
9	7,595186	12,32178	17,37767	16,99929	20,58578	18,6433	17,00101	-210,058	16,99889	16,99921	
10	7,658695	11,34934	15,29914	15,00299	17,80423	16,28814	15,00381	-163,195	15,00258	15,00259	
11	0,536591	0,266884	0,021628	0,00011	0,204687	0,093836	0,000168	12,95913	0,000107	0,000111	
12											

Fig. 5.24 Example of the Sknowinnov system in use

Regional assistant.xls [Tryb zgodności] - Microsoft Ex

I4 f_x -2,09847936034202

	A	B	C	D	E	F	G	H	I	J	K
1	0,00256	0,006594	-0,10829	-0,20816	-0,01802	-0,19671	-0,10588	-0,71092	-0,64902	-0,31989	
2	0,43246	0,538231	-1,6116	1,408161	-0,86668	-3,10118	1,147564	-21,4702	3,459216	1,578867	
3	0,566239	0,462212	2,647764	-0,34484	1,874737	4,162918	-0,11409	22,54443	2,253952	-0,47843	
4	-3,74103	-9,27863	-10,1114	-0,76462	-36,2689	-18,6255	-0,38632	-166,508	-2,09848	-0,84247	
5	-3,74927	-9,41858	-10,4782	-0,64738	-36,6597	-19,2264	-0,32585	-171,902	-1,74861	-0,68861	
6	7,457764	18,68079	20,5887	1,406546	72,94104	37,85388	0,709424	337,5781	3,832304	1,522803	
7	1;2	1;3	1;4	1;5	2;3	2;4	2;5	3;4	3;5	4;5	
8											

Fig. 5.25 Example of the Sknowinnov system in use

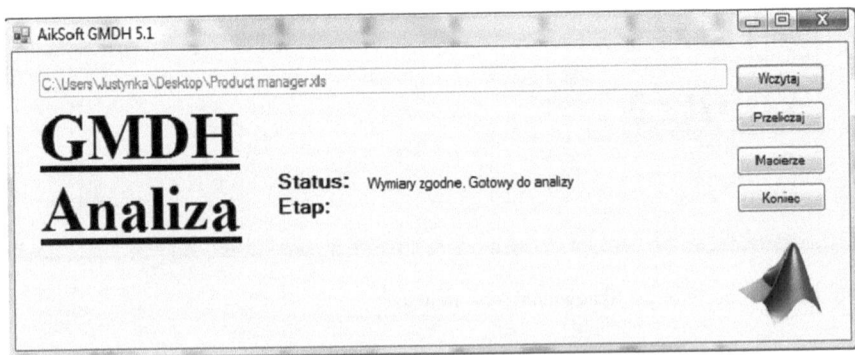

Fig. 5.26 Example of the Sknowinnov system in use

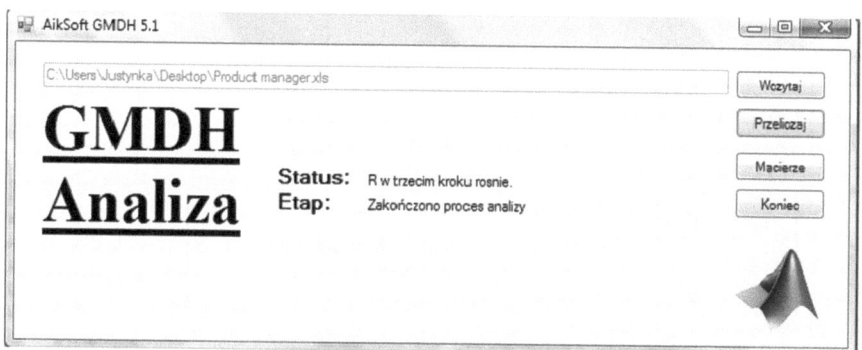

Fig. 5.27 Example of the Sknowinnov system in use

	A	B	C	D	E	F	G	H	I	J	K
1	16,00365	15,99977	15,99947	15,99981	16,00066	15,99973949	16,00055	15,62172	12,01531	-2,00782	
2	18,00637	18,00083	17,99973	18,00067	18,00036	17,99955561	18,0006	17,49376	12,68587	-6,05473	
3	20,00659	20,00032	19,99997	20,00001	20,00037	20,00005955	19,99988	19,34246	13,09543	-11,2912	
4	16,00531	15,99981	15,99946	16,00025	16,0005	15,9996998	16,00052	15,62062	12,01665	-2,00652	
5	17,00422	16,99915	16,99975	16,99978	16,99928	16,99994963	17	16,55961	12,37937	-3,88352	
6	16,00599	16,00067	16,00141	16,00111	15,99972	16,0013395	16,00071	15,62245	12,01705	-2,00828	
7	18,00572	18,0005	18,0004	17,99951	18,00098	18,00059856	17,99918	17,49499	12,68665	-6,05025	
8	19,00511	18,99884	18,99965	18,99971	18,99901	18,99991446	19,00015	18,42331	12,92571	-8,52028	
9	16,00348	15,99983	15,99943	15,9987	15,9994	15,99928476	15,99812	15,62165	12,01489	-2,00431	
10	23,0077	22,99993	22,99985	22,99992	23,00004	23,00003245	22,99995	22,06552	13,17085	-21,6795	
11	0,000309	3,37E-05	3,2E-05	3,45E-05	3,44E-05	3,05492E-05	4,18E-05	0,02995	0,314958	1,427301	
12											

Fig. 5.28 Example of the Sknowinnov system in use

	A	B	C	D	E	F	G	H	I	J	K
1	-3,7873	-7,38565	-9,6238	-13,4125	-7,92605	-10,0552	-17,4338	-0,2392	10,96574	1,135157	
2	-6,93728	3,401414	3,633641	5,030836	3,213497	3,412452	5,550736	5,281433	-49,2993	-2,28094	
3	8,766108	-0,80963	-0,55337	-1,15819	-0,51705	-0,24339	-0,83808	-4,17896	47,55554	3,075378	
4	-0,82566	-0,20199	-0,25554	-0,34306	-0,18132	-0,22981	-0,38165	-4,04677	63,02307	-3,34985	
5	-1,60048	-0,02394	-0,02898	-0,03722	-0,01444	-0,01934	-0,03027	-3,56447	56,71576	-3,48779	
6	2,39956	0,149988	0,168783	0,229865	0,112857	0,126144	0,208682	7,591217	-119,586	6,791992	
7	1;2	1;3	1;4	1;5	2;3	2;4	2;5	3;4	3;5	4;5	
8											

Fig. 5.29 Example of the Sknowinnov system in use

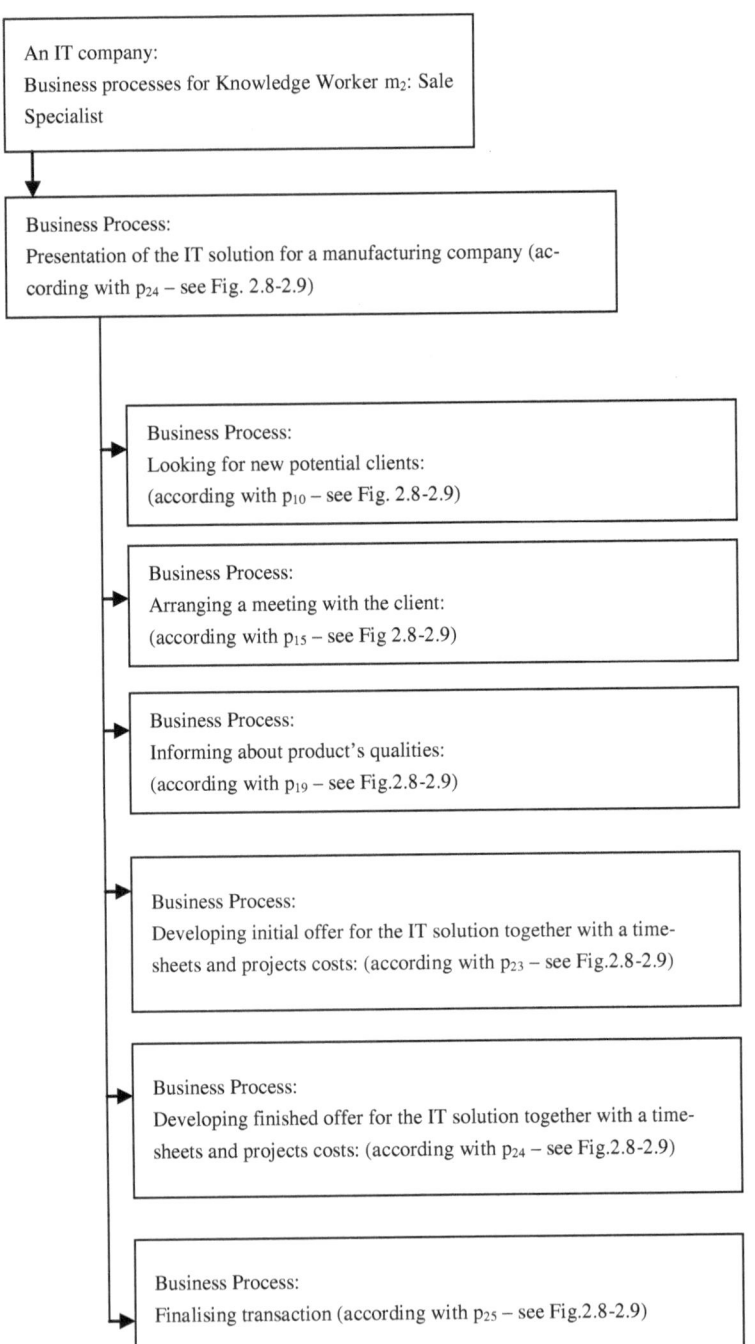

Fig. 5.30 Business processes in an IT company for a knowledge worker, m_2—sales specialist

Fig. 5.31 Examples of the Sknowinnov system in use

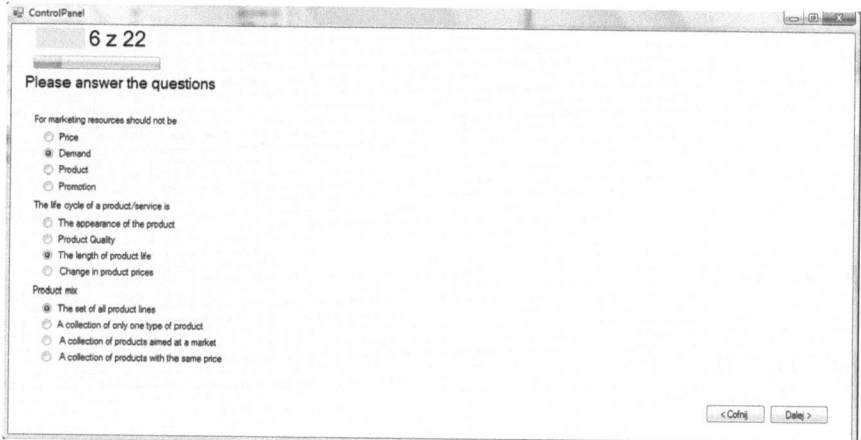

Fig. 5.32 Examples of the Sknowinnov system in use

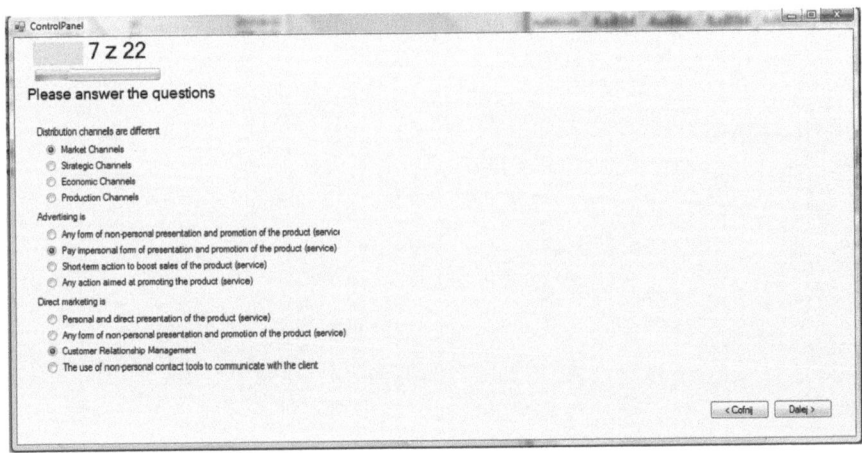

Fig. 5.33 Examples of the Sknowinnov system in use

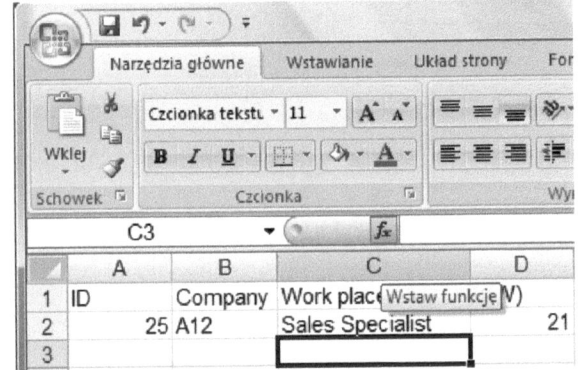

Fig. 5.34 Examples of the
Sknowinnov system in use

Since there was similarity in the values—the actual personnel usefulness func-tion and the predicted values based on the answer sheet—it was decided that this company should hire the employee as sales specialist.

This monograph examines the usefulness and the applicability of my decision-making model for selecting knowledge workers from a group of specialists in selling. The information presented is based on a real case study. The sections above presented a review of the appropriate research.

Reference

Patalas-Maliszewska, J. (2009). The concept of system supporting decision making enabling to asses and forecast of knowledge in SMEs—Research results. *Applied Computer Science, 5*(2), 27–41.

Conclusion

The capacity to manage knowledge and convert it into useful products and services is fast becoming the current primary executive skill. As a result, there has been a flurry of interest in IC, creativity, innovation, and learning within an organization. However, surprisingly little attention has been given to the management of dependence on the value of IC and innovation in companies.

This monograph was motivated by the actual need of a manager, who had a strong desire to improve his company's innovation level through appropriate knowledge worker selection. I began with a literature review of employee-selection methods and definitions of knowledge workers. Next, by empirical research conducted among Polish companies, I presented my polynomial models of decision making (the best polynomials) for individual knowledge workers—m1, m2, m3, m4, and m5. I established the Sknowinnov model, which allows a multi-criteria evaluation of the effectiveness of knowledge worker selection in a company.

Personnel planning is particularly important in terms of efficient management in a dynamic environment. The ability to select and use appropriate methods for planning employment should increase the rational use of human resource in the real economy. For an organization to succeed, management needs to operate at the level of strategic planning. The proposed method (Sknowinnov method) for assessing knowledge workers toward increasing a company's innovative capacity allows new employees to be selected on the basis of the experience of companies with similar activities (see test results) and a questionnaire for assessing new employees.

The Sknowinnov method can also be used in conjunction with other methods. It consists of reproducing aspects of the actual working situation and processes in terms of a model, which makes specific assumptions to improve their knowledge. With the current state of research, this method can be applied by adopting a reference model for the sales department for specific workplaces. The selection of employees using the proposed method is characterized by objectivity; it is methodical, uniform, fair, impartial, and professional. Using the personnel usefulness function should provide acquisition personnel with skilled staff, thereby ensuring the smooth functioning of the organization over time.

J. Patalas-Maliszewska, *Managing Knowledge Workers*, Management for Professionals, DOI 10.1007/978-3-642-36600-0_6, © Springer-Verlag Berlin Heidelberg 2013

An enterprising company functioning in a market economy has to implement changes in its systems of organization and management. In economic practice, making a decision in a company is conditioned by the actions of competitors and changing factors in the business environment, e.g., technical progress and the results of research. Because a competitive advantage accrues in those companies that effectively generate, maintain, and exploit knowledge with respect to their task domain and themselves, there is a need for a system to facilitate decision making at a strategic level in terms of the profitability of investing in staff knowledge.

Companies that recognize the necessity to plan and report on their knowledge value in the face of economic globalization and intensified competition have to choose the correct, most appropriate method (or tool). In striving to attain their main aim, which could be the improvement of certain chosen parameters within a specific time frame, enterprises need an advisory system for evaluating and forecasting their internal capital, especially IC.

Assessing the value of knowledge is a complicated task. The main sources of the complexity with this problem are as follows: operating under uncertain conditions; the multiple factors involved in making decisions (many parameters relate to the effectiveness of a given undertaking, and they have different degrees of influence on the final decision); and multiple levels of decision making (some parameters can be determined as a result of the aggregation of secondary parameters).

Managing strategic knowledge in an innovative company comprises a number of central issues, which are essential to an emerging company; they include the following:

- Understanding the strategic role of IC.
- Understanding innovation and innovativeness.
- Creating the right kind of management for cultivating and sharing IC.
- Monitoring and valuing IC.

The core aim of the present work is to act as a guide to creating a universal management model for strategic knowledge in an innovative company. The focus has been on describing a model of a knowledge worker-oriented company and creating a decision model for IC management in an innovative company. In particular, empirical research was carried out among companies that conform to the concrete model of enterprise. A software system for facilitating decision making at a strategic level in terms of the profitability of investing in staff knowledge was created; the designed method evaluates the effectiveness of investing in IC in a company (Sknowinnov method), and it makes use of the results of questionnaire-based research. The introduced Sknowinnov method allows for more possibilities in the area of knowledge profitability.

In addition to calculating investment profitability, this approach appears to be an excellent tool for an economic analysis of knowledge. The suggested IT tool for assessing knowledge workers relative to increasing the innovation in a company was based on my collected data. It connects the values of the personnel usefulness function for employees with the characteristics of innovation and indicators that allow an assessment of the rationality and effectiveness of knowledge. As a consequence, the present study may also allow an evaluation of knowledge itself.

Appendix 1: Evaluation Sheet for a Knowledge Worker in the Sales Area in an Innovative Company

1. For marketing resources should not be:
   - Price
   - Demand
   - Product
   - Promotion
2. The life cycle of a product/service is:
   - The appearance of the product
   - Product quality
   - The length of the product life
   - Change in product prices
3. Product mix:
   - The set of all product lines
   - A collection of only one type of product
   - A collection of products aimed at a market
   - A collection of products with the same price
4. Distribution channels are different:
   - Market channels
   - Strategic channels
   - Economic channels
   - Production channels
5. Advertising is:
   - Any form of nonpersonal presentation and promotion of the product (service)
   - Paying for an impersonal form of presentation and promotion of the product (service)
   - Short-term action to boost sales of the product (service)
   - Any action aimed at promoting the product (service)
6. Direct marketing is:
   - Personal and direct presentation of the product (service)
   - Any form of nonpersonal presentation and promotion of the product (service)
   - Customer relationship management
   - The use of nonpersonal contact tools to communicate with the client

J. Patalas-Maliszewska, *Managing Knowledge Workers*, Management for Professionals, DOI 10.1007/978-3-642-36600-0, © Springer-Verlag Berlin Heidelberg 2013

7. Sales promotion is:
   - Short-term action to boost sales of the product (service)
   - The planned long-term promotion of a product (service)
   - Measures to promote the product (service) conducted via the Internet
   - Measures to promote the product (service) conducted by telephone
8. Public relations is:
   - Promotion of products (services) in the media without permission
   - Planned promotion campaign in the media
   - The long-term promotion of products (services) in the media
   - Any action aimed at promoting the product (service)
9. Carrying out activities aimed at building a strategy for the company is impor-
   tant because:
   - Does not allow long-term development of the company in an industry
   - Anticipated change in the business environment
   - Does not allow development in conditions of increasing competition
   - Allows the elimination of the risk of misdiagnosis of business development
10. Asset-enterprise strength is not:
    - The possibility of extending the range
    - Good reputation with customers
    - Being recognized as a market leader
    - Experienced management team
11. Does the company intend to launch a new product on the market?
    - Yes
    - Now
    - I do not know
12. Does the company intend to change the user market?
    - Yes
    - Now
    - I do not know
13. Does the company want to introduce new sales channels?
    - Yes
    - Now
    - I do not know
14. Does the company want to enter new markets?
    - Yes
    - Now
    - I do not know
15. Does the customer have an exclusive supply provider?
    - Yes
    - Now
    - I do not know
16. Is the client sensitive to price changes?
    - Yes
    - Now
    - I do not know

17. Does the client use the supplier's Web site?
    - Yes
    - Now
    - I do not know
18. Is the customer satisfied with the work of the supplier's sales offices?
    - Yes
    - Now
    - I do not know
19. Is the customer satisfied with the terms of vendor contracts?
    - Yes
    - Now
    - I do not know
20. Is the customer kept informed about changes in the company?
    - Yes
    - Now
    - I do not know
21. I represent the interests of the client's in my own company
    - Occasionally
    - Sometimes
    - Often
    - Very often
    - Always
22. I maintain contacts with customers after the sale
    - Occasionally
    - Sometimes
    - Often
    - Very often
    - Always
23. I supplement knowledge about changes of product range in my company's
    - Occasionally
    - Sometimes
    - Often
    - Very often
    - Always
24. I inform customers about changes in the market
    - Occasionally
    - Sometimes
    - Often
    - Very often
    - Always
25. I supplement knowledge about changes in product mix at the customer
    - Occasionally
    - Sometimes
    - Often
    - Very often
    - Always

26. I prepare to talk to my customers
    - Occasionally
    - Sometimes
    - Often
    - Very often
    - Always
27. I lead discussions with clients
    - Occasionally
    - Sometimes
    - Often
    - Very often
    - Always
28. Number of years in a company. . . . .
29. An age. . . . .
30. The number of my ideas realized. . . . .
31. The value of my patents. . . . .
32. The number of my patents . . . .
33. The value of my copyright. . . . .
34. The number of my projects pending patent. . . . .
35. The number of my customers . . . .
36. The number of my regular customers . . . .
37. The number of my transactions (such as auction business documents, contracts, acquired clients)/month . . . .
38. I care more about
    - The feelings of people
    - Their rights
39. I am usually more comfortable with people
    - Who are gifted with imagination
    - Who are realists
40. A bigger compliment is to define someone as
    - Influencing other people
    - A rationally thinking person
41. If I do something together with many people, it is more important for me
    - To act in an acceptable manner
    - To find my own course of action
42. I am more irritated by
    - Theorists
    - Extreme practitioners
43. Higher praise should be given to someone
    - With vision
    - With common sense
44. With me, it is more for
    - My heart to rule my head
    - My head to rule my heart

45. I think a bigger mistake is
    - An excessive display of warm feelings
    - Not being simpatico
46. If I were a teacher, I would prefer to teach:
    - Theoretical subjects
    - Subjects based on important facts
47. Which word appeals to you more?
    - Compassion
    - Predictability
48. Which word appeals to you more?
    - Justice
    - Pity
49. Which word appeals to you more?
    - Production
    - Project
50. Which word appeals to you more?
    - Mild
    - Firm
51. Which word appeals to you more?
    - Indiscriminate
    - Critical
52. Which word appeals to you more?
    - Literal
    - Figurative
53. Which word appeals to you more?
    - Ingenious
    - Practical

Appendix 2: Guide for Using the Software System for Facilitating Decision Making at a Strategic Level in Terms of the Profitability of Investment in Knowledge Workers (Sknowinnov System)

The method for managing strategic knowledge in a company—the Sknowinnov method—uses the GMDH algorithm to predict the characteristics of innovation that will result through hiring knowledge workers. To verify the practical usefulness of this method, which was developed as a computer program, a series of tests have been designed. Implementing the software system facilitates decision making at a strategic level in terms of the profitability of investing in staff knowledge (Sknowinnov system).

This appendix contains the Quick Start Guide to the Sknowinnov system.

Startup and Operation of the Program

When the Sknowinnov system is started, the window title is displayed on the screen (see Fig. A.1).

The application window consists of the following elements (indicated in Fig. A.1):

- A—[Add] button: This allows a new company to be added. The next steps include a checklist of whether the company making the application meets the objectives and criteria for the reference model enterprises of small and medium-sized enterprises, as defined in this work. This leads to a number of tests completed by every employee in the sales department.
- B–[Edit] button: This position provides data analysis of the companies according with a reference model.
- C–[Delete] button: This allows the deletion of data relating to an enterprise.
- D–[Analysis] button: This provides data analysis.
- E–[Export] button: This allows the transfer of data to an Excel file.
- F–[F(W)->] button: This displays the value of the utility function for each employee in the company.
- G–[End] button: This allows the application to be exited.
- H–[Special] button: This allows data analysis to be performed on selected companies.
- I–[Filter] button: This allows data analysis using introduced criteria.

J. Patalas-Maliszewska, *Managing Knowledge Workers*, Management for Professionals, DOI 10.1007/978-3-642-36600-0, © Springer-Verlag Berlin Heidelberg 2013

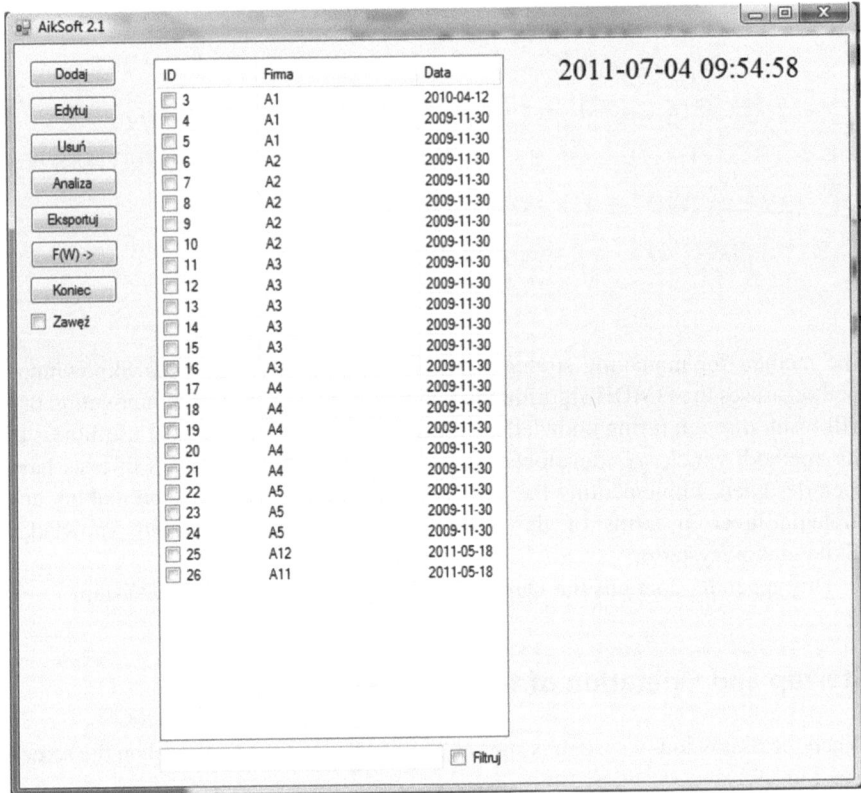

Fig. A.1 Window title of the program

A Company

Selecting [Add] position in the window title allows a new business to be added. It permits verification as to whether it is possible to carry out the forecast efficiency for selecting employees by the enterprise. The decision-making procedure for selecting knowledge workers is appropriate only for a knowledge worker-oriented company (see Sect. 3.2.2).

After starting the program, the [Add] window appears, where the user defines the business (Fig. A.2). The user selects the appropriate areas using the mouse.

The software user has the option of selecting the area in the company where he or she works (Fig. A.2) and the actions to be performed (Figs. A.2, A.3, A.4, A.5, and A.6).

Fig. A.2 Window for "Company name"

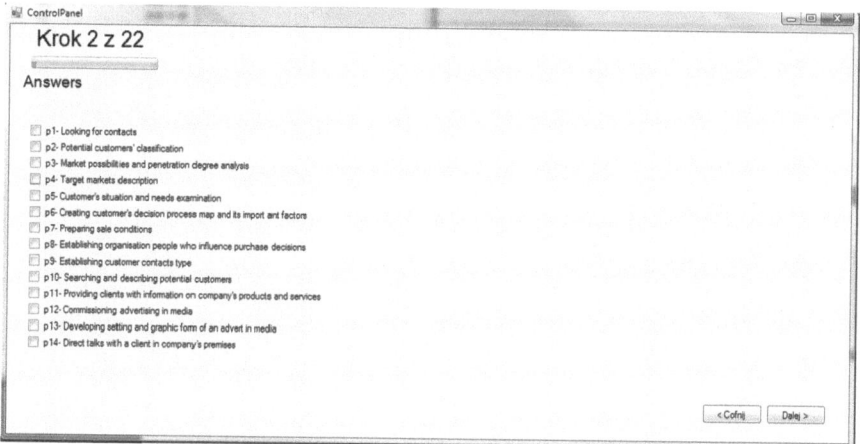

Fig. A.3 Window "Answers"

Tests to Obtain the Value of the Personnel Usefulness Function

To obtain the value of the personnel usefulness function for each employee in the sales area in a company, the employee has to answer the following questions (Figs. A.7 A.8, A.9, A.10, A.11, A.12, A.13, A.14, A.15, A.16, and A.17).

User-defined data obtained from the value of the personnel usefulness function for personnel and its components are entered (Figs. A.18 and A.19).

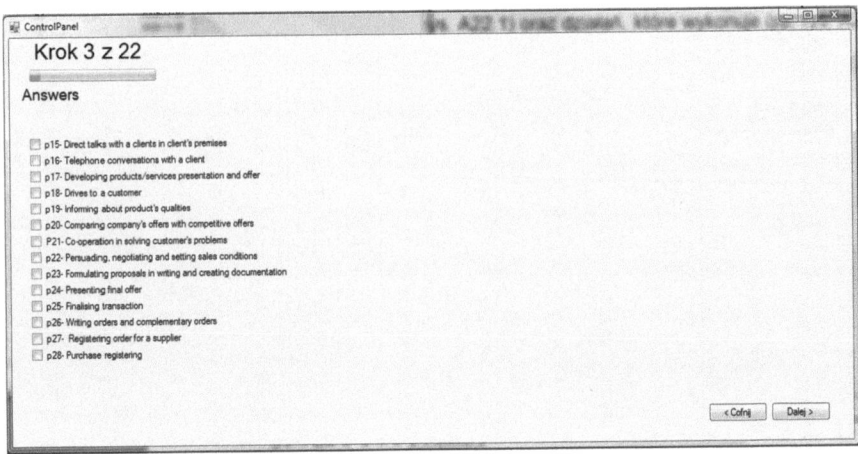

Fig. A.4 Window "Answers"

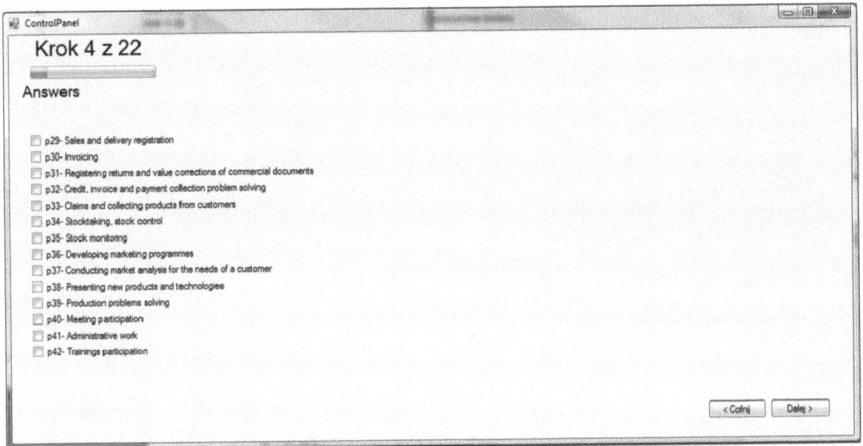

Fig. A.5 Window "Answers"

Forecast Value of the Personnel Usefulness Function According to the Level of Innovation in a Company

The "prediction" (Fig. A.20) allows the user to forecast the value of the personnel usefulness function according to the level of innovation in a company by means of the resulting decision-making model, which links selected indicators of innovation with the real values of this function. The GMDH algorithm applied to the objective selection method involves creating an employee database containing the data recorded during observation of the test object (a company). The base rates of innovation and values for the personnel usefulness function were established

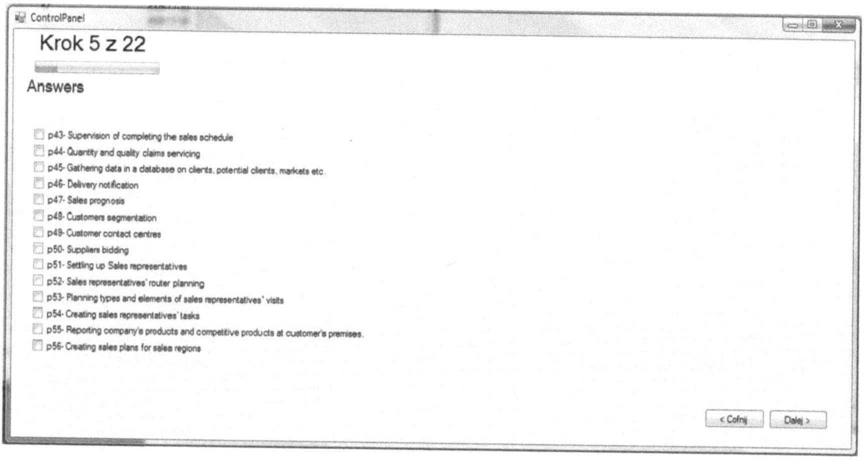

Fig. A.6 Window "Answers"

Fig. A.7 Window "Please answer the question"

based on the experience of 10 Polish companies. Surveys were conducted among Polish enterprises that fitted the model reference.

The prediction button of the program includes the following options (Fig. A.21):

• [Load] button—allows the selection of data from an Excel file (Fig. A.22).
• [Matrix] button—allows the data to be shown

There is the possibility of introducing a new database. Consequently, a new decision model is created, as defined by the employee based on the developed procedure.

Option [Converts]: this allows the forecast value of the personnel usefulness function to be read for the new potential employee under the applicable decision-making model and parameter values entered by the user. The [Converts] button

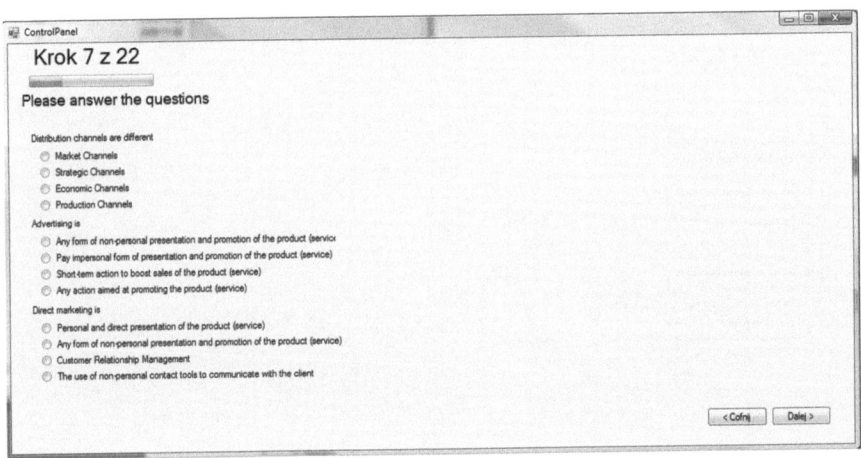

Fig. A.8 Window "Please answer the question"

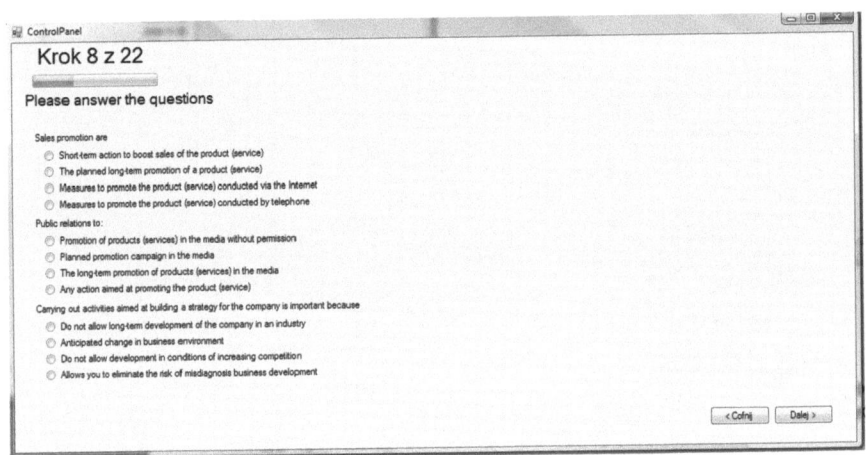

Fig. A.9 Window "Please answer the question"

includes the [Export] function, which allows the transfer of data to an Excel file to supply the predicted values for selected parameters (any user) (Fig. A.23). The method of forecasting and interpretation of the results are discussed with the examples in third and fourth chapter.

The Excel file provides the opportunity of presenting the next steps defined in the employee-selection procedures (Chap. 5) (Figs. A.24 and A.25).

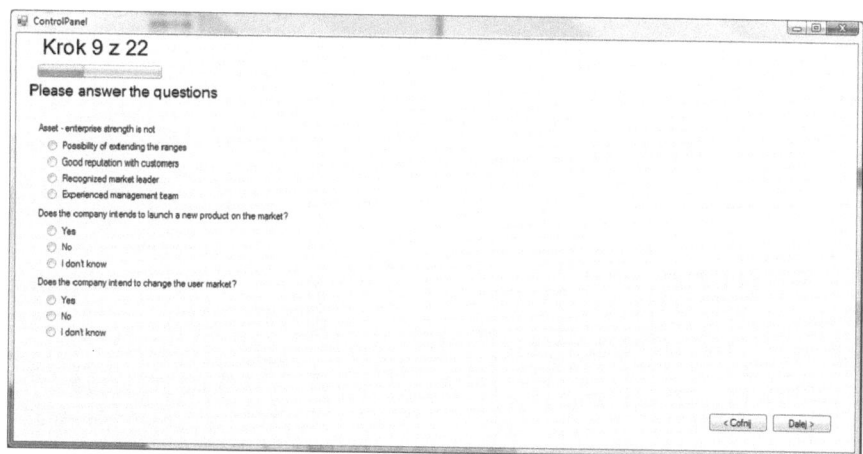

Fig. A.10 Window "Please answer the question"

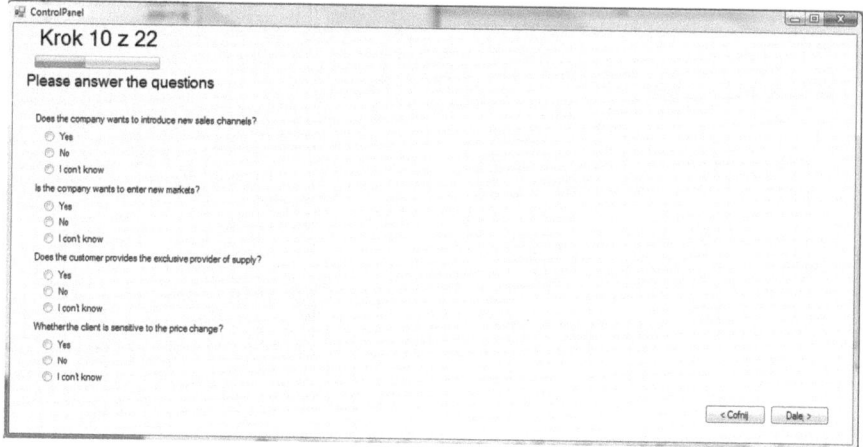

Fig. A.11 Window "Please answer the question"

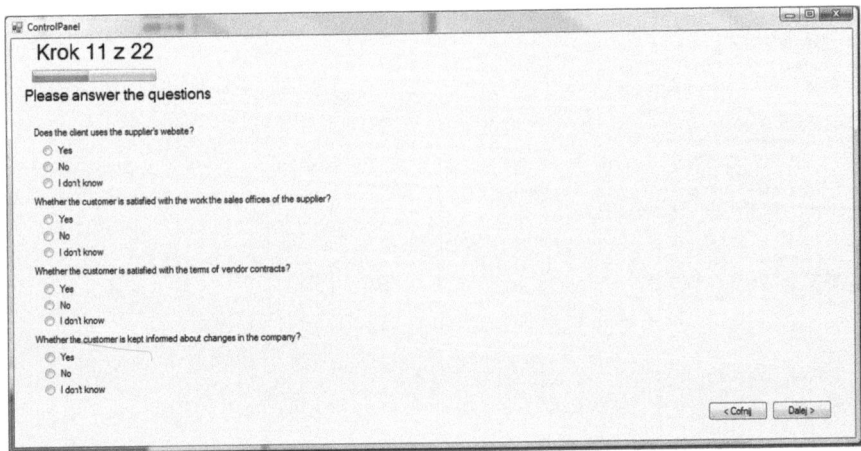

Fig. A.12 Window "Please answer the question"

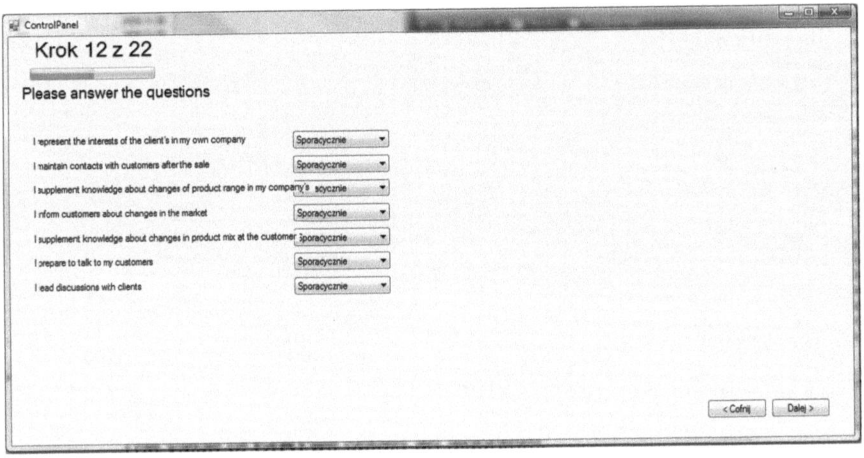

Fig. A.13 Window "Please answer the question"

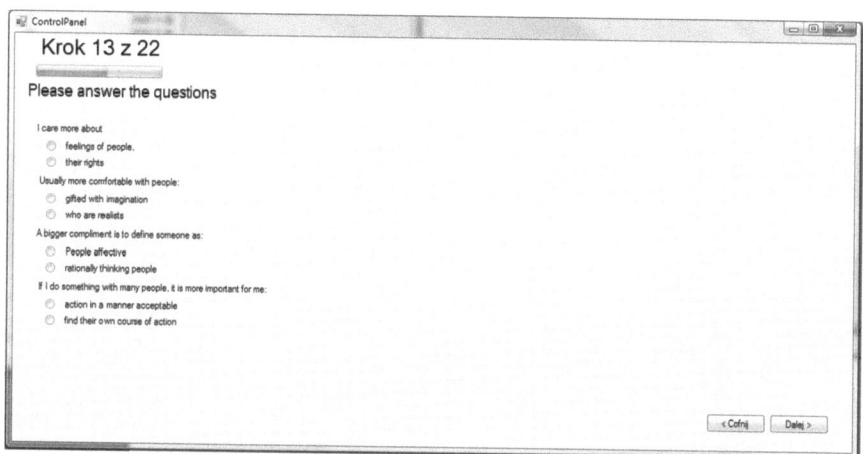

Fig. A.14 Window "Please answer the question"

Fig. A.15 Window "Please answer the question"

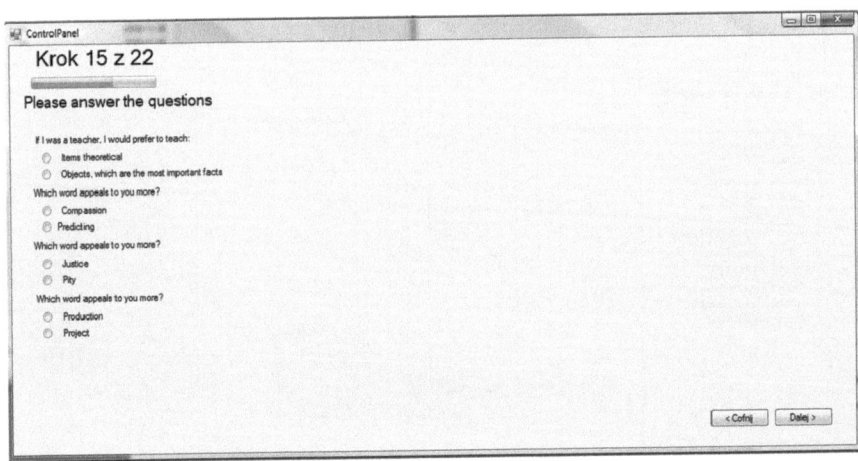

Fig. A.16 Window "Please answer the question"

Fig. A.17 Window "Please answer the question"

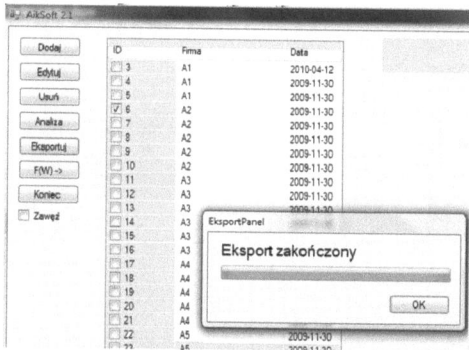

Fig. A.18 Window "Value of the personnel usefulness function" for each employee in a company

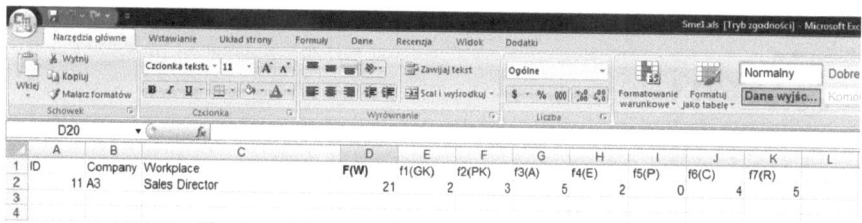

Fig. A.19 Window "Value of the personnel usefulness function" for each employee in a company

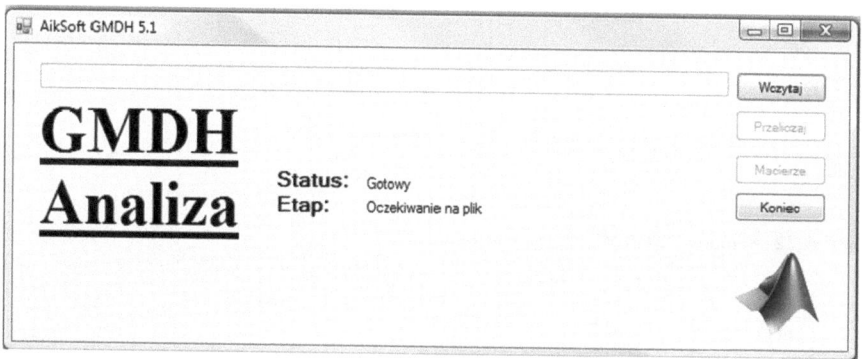

Fig. A.20 Window "Prediction"

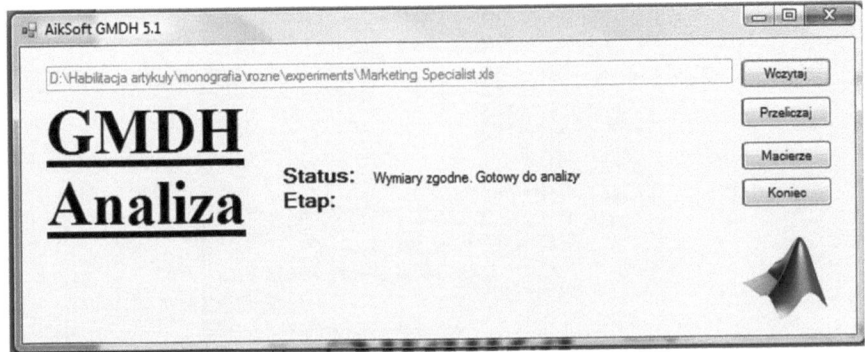

Fig. A.21 Window "Prediction"

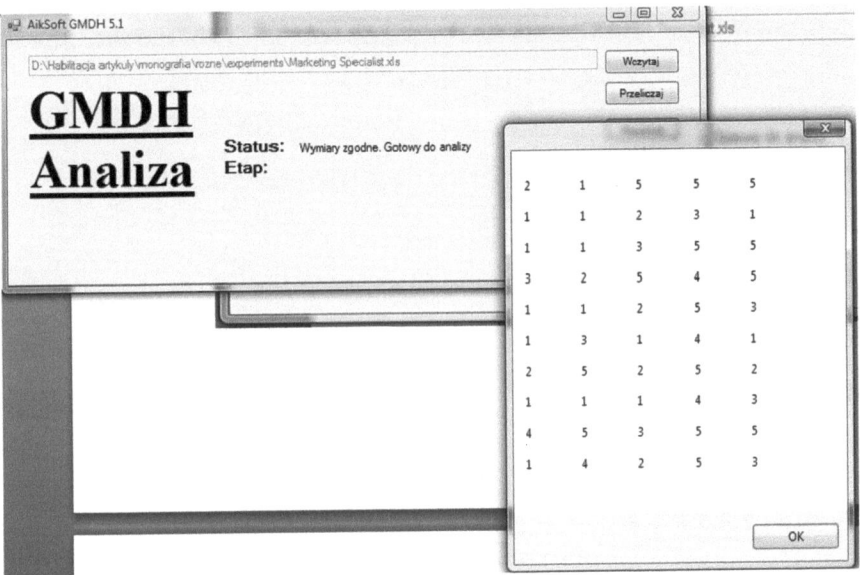

Fig. A.22 Window "Matrix"

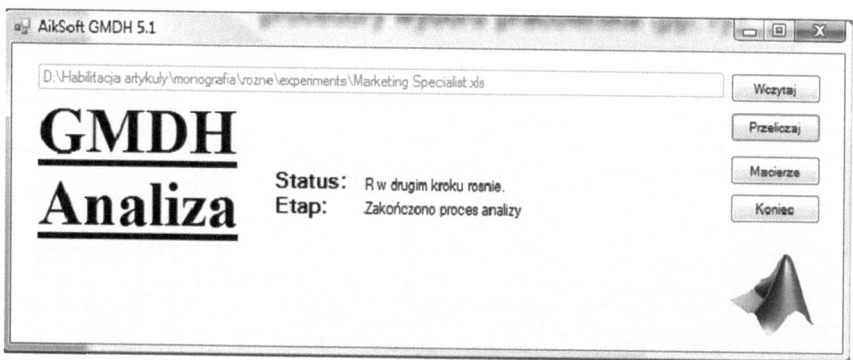

Fig. A.23 Window "Prediction"

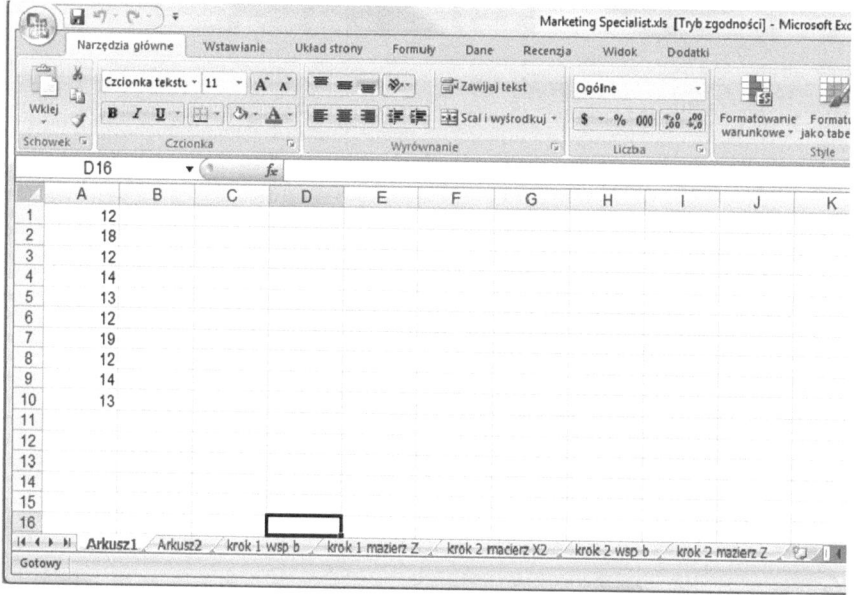

Fig. A.24 Window "Prediction" in Excel

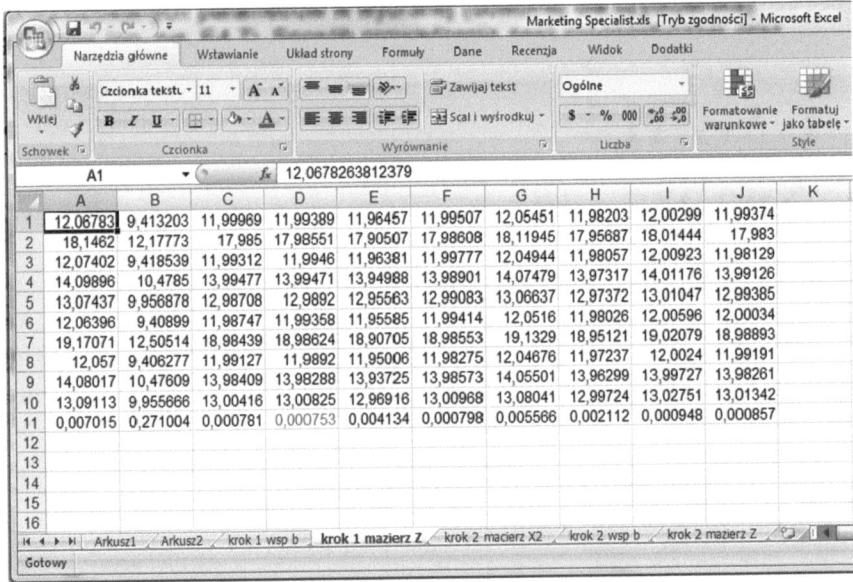

Fig. A.25 Window "Prediction" in Excel